THE SECRET OF SHELTER ISLAND

Money and What Matters

ALEXANDER GREEN

WILEY

John Wiley & Sons, Inc.

Published by John Wiley & Sons, Inc., Hoboken, New Jersey.
Published simultaneously in Canada.

For general information on our other products and services or for technical support, please contact our Customer Care Department within the United States at (800) 762–2974, outside the United States at (317) 572–3993 or fax (317) 572–4002.

Wiley also publishes its books in a variety of electronic formats. Some content that appears in print may not be available in electronic books. For more information about Wiley products, visit our web site at www.wiley.com.

Library of Congress Cataloging-in-Publication Data:

Green, Alexander, 1958–
    The secret of shelter island : money and what matters / Alexander Green.
        p.   cm.
    Includes bibliographical references and index.
    ISBN 978-0-470-48228-5 (cloth)
        1. Money—Philosophy.   2. Finance, Personal.   I. Title.
    HG220.3.G74 2009
    332.024—dc22
                                                            2009007446

Printed in the United States of America
10 9 8 7 6 5 4 3 2 1

For Hannah and David

Money has yet to make anyone rich.

—Seneca

CONTENTS

PART FOUR   THE SEARCH FOR MEANING   **185**

PREFACE

After more than 25 years of virtually uninterrupted prosperity, the U.S. economy has hit a rough patch.

As I write, jobless claims are at a 27-year high. Consumer confidence is at an all-time low. Credit is tight. Business investment and personal spending have plunged. Housing is in a death spiral. The U.S. auto industry is on the verge of collapse. And the stock market just experienced its worst year since 1931.

Welcome to The Great Recession.

There's nothing funny, of course, about losing your job, getting evicted, or watching your net worth plummet. Economic downturns bring pain and suffering. There will be plenty of belt-tightening—and sober reflection—in the months ahead.

But to the extent recessions shake up the status quo and force us to examine our goals and priorities, they also offer enormous opportunities.

This book is meant to aid in that process. *The Secret of Shelter Island* is partly about money. But it is also about putting it—and the rest of your life—in perspective.

There has rarely been a better time to do so. We are experiencing a financial slump unlike any in modern times. Virtually every investor has seen his net worth get a serious haircut.

How did we get here? There is plenty of blame to go around, starting with reckless lenders, overly ambitious borrowers, unethical CEOs, feckless investors, and shortsighted policy makers.

Too many were chasing the fast buck, took momentary leave of their senses, or abandoned their basic values. This is especially true on Wall Street. Vanguard Founder John Bogle hits the nail on the head in his book *Enough*:

"Not knowing what *enough* is subverts our professional values. It makes salespersons of those who should be fiduciaries of the investments entrusted to them. It turns a system that should be built on trust into one with counting as its foundation. Worse, this confusion about *enough* leads us astray in our larger lives. We chase the false rabbits of success; we too often bow down at the altar of the transitory and finally meaningless and fail to cherish what is beyond calculation, indeed eternal."

In many ways, *enough* is a central message of this book. Even during this historic downturn, most Americans have ample material wealth. (Covering our basic needs just doesn't take that much.) But how about the immaterial?

What is your animating purpose? How are you spending your time? What are you living for?

Many of us—perhaps especially those with a newfound hole in their retirement account, financial plan, or tuition fund—are reappraising these questions now.

This book may help you see—or consider—things differently. It consists primarily of essays I wrote for *Spiritual Wealth,* a weekly e-letter that seeks "The Road Map to a Rich Life." If you're a new reader, welcome. If you're a regular reader, welcome back.

The Secret of Shelter Island is arranged around four central themes: A Rich Mind, What Matters Most, Attitudes and Gratitude, and The Search for Meaning. My objective here is to share some insights about "the big questions"—and perhaps provide a bit of inspiration, something we could all use in a world that bombards us with sad and tragic news.

If you're like me, you're tired of hearing about wild-eyed terrorists, drug-addled celebrities, ethically challenged businessmen and crooked politicians. The national media delivers a daily dose of heartbreak, misery, and cynicism. Much of what we watch and read each day is depressing, even rattling.

I wrote these essays as an antidote. They consist solely of ideas I've found particularly inspiring, elevating, or ennobling.

Over the last thirty years, I've spent a great deal of time studying history, philosophy, psychology, science and religion, saving and highlighting virtually everything I read. This project gave me the opportunity to revisit those classic works and cite some of the best minds and ideas of all time.

You'll notice that these pages lean heavily on quotes and sources from antiquity. Why? When it comes to wisdom about how to live your life, the best ideas are not new. As Ralph Waldo Emerson said, "All my best thoughts were stolen by the ancients."

Second, authoritative historical sources give more heft to anyone's point of view. I've found you don't get much opposition to ideas attributed to Cicero, Aristotle, or Epictetus. (Who really wants to argue with Marcus Aurelius?)

Judging by my mailbag, there is a great thirst out there for this kind of knowledge. Writers are always hearing from their readers, of course. But even in the glory days of the last bull market— or the depths of the previous bear—I never received an avalanche like this.

Readers told me these essays inspired them, motivated them, caused them to end a bad relationship, start a new career, forgive an old grudge, or spend a moment appreciating their incredible good fortune, whatever their current financial status.

They sent me books, poems, photographs, speaking invitations, and handwritten letters, some several pages long.

I was overwhelmed with the response. Not just emotionally, but physically. My publisher estimates that we received over 10,000 emails from readers in the first few months alone. It was simply not possible to respond to them all. Especially since, except for a copy editor who gives my columns the once-over for grammatical and typographical errors, I had no real staff for this project. My primary occupation is logging several thousand words of investment commentary each week. *Spiritual Wealth* is just a sideline, one that my publisher likes to remind me has never produced a penny of revenue.

Still, I enjoyed researching and writing these pieces—and learned a lot in the process. Now I'm pleased to share them with you.

And I think the moment is right. Given recent events, this is a particularly opportune time to consider the innate connection between money, values, and *the pursuit of the good life*.

ACKNOWLEDGMENTS

I could never have written this book without the fine words and great ideas of some of history's best thinkers. We are all truly standing on the shoulders of giants.

I would also like to thank several more contemporary writers who have helped shape my views, including Karen Armstrong, Joseph Campbell, Huston Smith, Thich Nhat Hanh, Laurence G. Boldt, Jack Kornfield, Eckhart Tolle, John Horgan, Martin Seligman, Paul Kurtz, Richard Dawkins, Daniel Dennett, Mihaly Csikszentmihalyi, Carl Sagan, Charles Murray, Nathaniel Branden, Stephen Jay Gould, Sam Harris, David McCullough, Christopher Hitchens, Gregg Easterbrook, George Will, Steven R. Covey, Matthew Kelly, Daniel Gilbert, Michael Shermer, James Hollis, and Timothy Ferris.

Particular thanks to British author Bryan Magee for his excellent memoir *Confessions of a Philosopher.*

(I would also like to state, for the record, that I hate Bill Bryson. All writers should. If you don't know why, read everything he's written.)

Many thanks to Mrs. Gant, my high school English teacher, who inspired me—and paid me the biggest compliment of my

17-year-old life—when she asked whether I "planned to do anything" with my writing.

(And to the career counselor at Furman University who suggested I had a better chance of playing third base for the Yankees than earning a living wage as a writer, let me add—with all due respect—*nah nah nah boo boo.*)

It has been my exceptional good fortune to work with Julia Guth, Bill Bonner, Mark Ford, Myles Norin, and my other colleagues, mentors, and good friends at Agora Publishing. (Many thanks to Steven King, Alex Wissel, Christina Olson, Alex Williams, Chris Matthai, Katherine Schildt, and Matt Weinschenk for putting up with me every day.) What a great bunch of people and inspiring place to work, even though our marketing remains minimal, constrained, and hopelessly understated.

Thanks, too, to my publishers and editors at John Wiley & Sons, including Debra Englander and Kelly O'Connor, who reviewed this manuscript and recommended some important changes and clarifications.

I would also like to thank my regular readers at The Oxford Club, Investment U, and *Spiritual Wealth*. Without an audience, a writer is just an opinionated crank. (We're opinionated cranks anyway, of course.)

Let me doff my hat to my good friends Mark Skousen and Rob Fix. Our many private debates—I'm still wiping the spittle off my windshield, Rob—helped sharpen my own views on many philosophical and religious matters.

Special thanks to my parents Braxton and Judith Green who, through their positive spirit and attitude toward life, taught me the best things I know. They and my wife, Karen; daughter, Hannah; and son, David are my greatest treasure—and my real source of wealth.

INTRODUCTION

When I stepped down from the podium in Phoenix, the applause from the audience of more than 600 was still ringing in my ears.

Readers were in high spirits. And why not? It was 2007 and for five straight years we had enjoyed a smooth rise in stock and bond prices.

Markets were good. Our portfolios were flush with profits. And my investment letter, *The Oxford Club Communique,* had been singled out by the independent *Hulbert Financial Digest* as one of the top letters in the country for five-year performance for two years running.

This didn't stop a nattily dressed older gentleman from button-holing me in the lobby with some choice words, however.

"Money, money, money, money," he said with rising emphasis, stabbing a finger toward my chest. "You've made me a lot of money over the years. But let me ask, do you ever think about *anything* else?"

At first I thought he was kidding. He wasn't. He just stood there in front of me, wide-eyed.

I'm used to getting feedback—both positive and negative—from readers who follow my investment advice. But I'd never had one baldly suggest that I was obsessed with money to the exclusion of everything else.

And he was dead serious. He stood there, patiently waiting for my response.

Do I ever think about anything *other* than money? How do you answer a question like that?

I remember wondering what had prompted the question. After all, we'd only just met. He knew me solely from my writing and lectures. Then it dawned on me . . .

For the previous seven years, I had dutifully churned out eight investment columns and articles a week—over 400 a year—with endless commentary on interest rates, currencies, stocks, bonds, commodities, mutual funds, hedge funds, convertibles, annuities, options, futures, diversification, asset allocation, takeovers, share buybacks, trailing stops, hot IPOs, how to increase returns, lower risks, reduce costs, minimize taxes, and so on.

Most of my pieces are short. And I try to keep them light and entertaining. Yet there was no denying that the primary subject of each of my previous 3,000 or so columns—not to mention every lecture, radio and television appearance—was exactly the same: money. How to make it. How to save it. How to invest it. How to multiply it.

I make no apologies for this, incidentally.

In more ways than I can enumerate, money is important. We all want to better our lives and our children's lives. We have a natural desire to experience the best that life has to offer. We want to live in good neighborhoods. Travel to new places. Try different things. Send our kids and grandkids to better schools. These things, you may have noticed, take money.

Money grants you the power to make important choices in your life. As I emphasized in my last book *The Gone Fishin' Portfolio* (John Wiley & Sons, Inc., 2008), financial independence is a worthwhile goal. It enables you to do what you want, where you want, with whom you want.

Still, I've never believed that getting, saving, spending, and investing are the most important things in life. Yet apparently I had created this impression with at least one reader—and probably more.

He remained steadfast in front of me, awaiting my reply. But he didn't get one—not a good one, anyway—until I began writing a new column a few weeks later, one he had inadvertently inspired.

When I broached the idea of a new "more meaningful" writing project with my publisher, Julia Guth, she seemed open-minded.

"What will these columns be about?"

I told her they would touch on money, but also things more important than money.

She looked intrigued, but skeptical. We're financial publishers. Our product is investment research and analysis, not musings about "the good life."

"But what are you going to say?" she persisted.

"I don't know yet," I confessed. "I'll have to write a few to find out."

She gave me a sideways glance. "You're not going to pull a Jerry Seinfeld on me and write about *nothing* are you?"

I assured her that, at the very least, each column would be about *something*. About what, exactly? I still wasn't sure.

Nor had I considered what to call a column by an investment analyst, written primarily for business and financial readers, dealing only tangentially with money.

Fortunately, a title popped into my head almost immediately: *True Wealth*. Everyone understands the pursuit of financial wealth. I would write about combining that with nonmaterial blessings too. *True wealth*.

It was perfect. There was only one small problem. My friend and colleague Steve Sjuggerud already owned the *True Wealth* trademark. He writes an investment letter by that name. (A good one, incidentally.) But it's about money, not things more important than money.

So what would I call this new column, one that wasn't devoted exclusively to financial matters? At some point I realized that if I wasn't writing about material wealth, I should just call it *Spiritual Wealth*.

My publisher, a spiritual sort (if I may say so), loved the title. But she was The Lone Ranger. Most everyone else in my office was negative, confused, or skeptical. None of them, however, suggested a better name.

A few days before kickoff, I was chatting with fellow editor Eric Frye at a company cocktail party. I told him about my latest project.

"*Spiritual Wealth?*" he asked in amazement. "Man, I wouldn't use *that* word."

"You mean *spiritual?*" I said.

"Yeah," he said with a laugh. "That's *dynamite.*"

I was beginning to have reservations. Why *was* this word so controversial?

It didn't take long to find out. As soon as we announced *Spiritual Wealth*—before we published a single column—I began receiving letters from regular readers who told me in no uncertain terms that they weren't about to listen to me—an investment analyst, for Pete's sake—lecture them about *spiritual matters.*

I had no intention of doing any such thing. But they never discovered that. The word carries certain connotations and their minds were made up.

Fortunately, these letters were a distinct minority. The vast majority of respondents loved having an opportunity to ruminate about what I call "The Great Ideas." In just a few weeks, we received thousands of testimonials.

At financial conferences, I began receiving ten comments about *Spiritual Wealth* for every comment about my other writing projects—the ones that actually pay the bills—combined.

People really are passionate about hearing and discussing these ideas.

And the letters kept pouring in. Many asked whether we intended to compile these essays into a book. Quite frankly, we hadn't. But readers asked so frequently, I began thinking it might be a good idea.

Most of us devote a substantial percentage of our waking hours to making, spending or having *more*. The desire to accumulate is natural, of course. But when a bigger bank balance—or the things it can buy—becomes our animating purpose, disappointment generally follows.

The Secret of Shelter Island is about recognizing the importance of money, but also the primacy of honoring and fighting for your highest potential, living the life you want, doing work you enjoy, paying attention to your highest goals and values.

Material wealth alone doesn't bring lasting satisfaction. And neither will nonmaterial blessings if you're wondering where you're going to get this month's rent. But combine a sensible approach to money with good choices about nonfinancial matters and the result is the best of all worlds.

That is the essential idea in these essays. Each one was written to stand alone, however, so feel free to skip around if you're so inclined.

Oh, and to the gentleman in Phoenix who wanted to know whether I ever think about *anything* besides money, let me just say yes—and thanks for asking.

PART ONE

A RICH MIND

By the time we reach adulthood, we have all developed a specific attitude toward—and relationship with—money.

This is especially true in my case. For the past 24 years, thinking about money has been my full-time job.

I spent 16 years as a research analyst, investment advisor, and portfolio manager. And in the eight years since I retired from Wall Street, I've been living what I call "the second half of my life," writing about world financial markets.

From an early age we're taught that the best things in life are free, that money can't buy happiness, that it can't buy love . . . and so forth. These thoughts are commonplace because they're true.

But that's not the whole story.

Money is the most egalitarian force in society, bestowing power on whoever holds it. It gives you the freedom to make important choices in your life. No one is truly free who is a slave to his job, his creditors, his circumstances, or his overhead.

Money may not buy happiness, but it sure steamrolls a whole lot of problems. As essayist Logan Pearsall Smith pointed out, "There are few sorrows, however poignant, in which a good income is of no avail."

Money also makes it easier to relax, to experience peace of mind. As author Tom Robbins notes, "There's a certain Buddhistic calm that comes from having money in the bank."

Overcoming money worries allows you to get on with your life and focus on the people and activities you love. To pretend this isn't so can be a form of denial, a sort of spiritual snobbery. Or it may mean that a lifetime of comfortable living has blinded us to the hardships that exist without it.

Money is freedom. It's power, in the best sense. It allows you to support worthy causes and help those in need. It enables you to spend your life the way you want.

Of course, it would probably take a lot of money for you to have and do *everything* you want. That may not be possible. More importantly, it may not be desirable.

As J. Brotherton said, "My riches consist not in the extent of my possessions, but in the fewness of my wants."

Once you start accumulating a bit of money, in fact, you're faced with a new set of problems and responsibilities. You have to grow and protect it. You have to manage risk, stay ahead of inflation and the taxman. You have to decide whom to give it to and when.

These issues were the subject of my previous book, *The Gone Fishin' Portfolio: Get Wise, Get Wealthy . . . and Get On With Your Life.*

In this book, I want to share a more personal philosophy of money . . . and of life.

What does money mean to you? What are you working for, saving for? How are you managing your relationship with money? How important is it in your life? What is it giving you? What is it costing you?

These are deeply personal issues. No one can simply hand you the answers. But it never hurts to consider the questions.

■ Are You Suffering From Affluenza?

In his 1997 film *Affluenza,* producer John de Graaf claims there is a virus loose in society that threatens our wallets, our friendships, our families, our communities, and our environment.

Each year it costs us hundreds of billions of dollars, wastes our precious time, ruins our health, and adversely affects our quality of life. What is affluenza, exactly?

De Graff defines it as "a painful, contagious, socially-transmitted condition of overload, debt, anxiety and waste resulting from the dogged pursuit of more."

He argues that too many of us are working ourselves to death to accumulate an endless array of goods and services we don't really need.

This creates stress. Stress, in turn, creates health problems, including headaches, stomachaches, ulcers, depression, even heart attacks.

Medical research shows that people in industrial nations lose more years from disability and premature death due to stress-related illnesses than other ailments.

Affluenza drives up healthcare costs, tears at the fabric of families, and shortens our stay on the right side of the daisies.

Before you mistake me for the national scold, however, let me make a couple of confessions.

First off, I'm a libertarian at heart. I realize that personal consumption—roughly two-thirds of all economic activity—drives the economy. Moreover, if someone really wants to devote his life to accumulating more, more, more, that's his right.

As John Maynard Keynes put it, "It is better that a man should tyrannize over his bank balance than over his fellow citizens."

(Although, personally, I've never met anyone who obtained lasting satisfaction with a Visa or Mastercard.)

Second, I'm not immune to the occasional bout of affluenza myself. I rarely pass a bookstore or record shop, for example, without poking my head inside. And whenever I leave Barnes & Noble, the clerk at the register always asks the same thing:

"Would you like us to double-bag that for you?"

We all have to consume to survive, of course. But Madison Avenue is right there beside us, aiding us, abetting us . . . giving us a not-so-subtle push.

Marketers want to convince us that our lives would be so much better if we would only just drive this car, drink this lite beer, use this antiwrinkle cream, or fly these friendly skies.

Every day we are bombarded: billboards, Internet banners, TV and radio commercials, newspaper and magazine ads. You can't even get away at a public beach. Single-engine planes criss-cross the sky trailing banners, "Joe's Crab Shack: All You Can Eat $17.99" or "2-for-1 Drinks All Day at Bennigan's."

Advertisers are getting more sophisticated, too. The new science of neuromarketing is designed to help retailers unlock the subconscious thoughts, feelings, and desires that drive our purchasing decisions.

Using magnetic resonance imaging scanners to record brain activity in minute detail, marketers now measure how their products affect the brain's pleasure centers. In short, they are creating products and advertising that stimulate the production of dopamine.

And it works. Today psychologists routinely talk about "retail therapy," where consumers shop just to get a short-term high to ward off boredom or the blues.

How do we resist?

First by recognizing our limits, both financial and material. After all, it really doesn't really take a lot of money to meet our needs.

Many of the other things we covet don't hold our attention long. Recognize that and you may conclude that they aren't worth the time and trouble it takes to acquire them.

As the philosopher Bertrand Russell wrote, "The man who acquires easily things for which he feels only a moderate desire concludes that the attainment of desire does not bring happiness. . . . He forgets that to be without some of the things you want is an indispensable part of happiness."

A well-lived life cannot just be about competing against others for resources. He who dies with the most toys *doesn't* win.

As Laurence G. Boldt writes in *The Tao of Abundance,*

The psychology of plenty differs fundamentally from the psychology of scarcity. If I view my life as a struggle to sustain my existence in an unfriendly world, then intimidation, competitiveness, and greed make sense. If I view life itself as a gift, attitudes of praise, thanksgiving and responsibility naturally follow.

It's only human to want to better our material conditions, of course. But the relentless quest for more often undermines our quality of life. Successful lives are built not bought. And an over-consumptive lifestyle ultimately limits our choices.

As Russell said, "It is preoccupation with possessions, more than anything else, that prevents us from living freely and nobly."

Curing affluenza means dropping the chains of mindless consumption. It means recognizing that lives based on having are less free than those based on doing or being.

Wise men and women have known this for millennia.

In 400 B.C.E., the Greek philosopher Diogenes taught that no man needed much—and that we shouldn't complain of material loss. He once went to Athens with his slave Manes, who ran away. Diogenes shrugged off his ill fortune saying, "If Manes can live without Diogenes, why not Diogenes without Manes?"

In *It's All In Your Head,* Stephen M. Pollan and Mark Levine relate another story about the famous ascetic:

Diogenes is sitting on the side of the road eating his simple meal of porridge. A court philosopher sees him and comes over to chat. "You know, Diogenes, if you learned to play up to the king like the rest of us, you wouldn't have to live on porridge." Diogenes doesn't even glance up from his bowl; he just says, "If you learned to live on porridge, you wouldn't have to play up to the king."

Reasonable, affordable consumption means less struggle, less debt, less hassles, less stress.

It also grants us more time—and with it the opportunity for new experiences, better relationships, and greater personal freedom.

As Oscar Wilde said, "The true perfection of man lies not in what man has, but in what man is." ∎

■ Why Money Won't Get You to "Level Three"

In the Declaration of Independence, Thomas Jefferson argued that life, liberty, and the pursuit of happiness are our inalienable rights.

You have life and more liberty than your ancestors could possibly have imagined. Not just freedom from tyrants and feudal lords, but freedom from backbreaking labor, forced conscription, arranged marriages, widespread banditry and injustice, religious persecution, economic privation, and the threat of dozens of now-curable diseases.

Happiness, on the other hand, is a little trickier.

Notice that Jefferson was wise enough to say we don't have a right to happiness itself, just the pursuit of it. After all, it can be elusive . . . especially Level Three.

According to Daniel Nettle, a lecturer in Psychology at the University of Newcastle in Britain and the author of *Happiness: The Science Behind Your Smile,* there are three levels of happiness.

Level One is the happiness of momentary feelings. This is the enjoyment we take in a good movie, a game of tennis, or a meal spent in the company of friends or family. This type of happiness is immediate but transient. Whenever you experience joy or pleasure, you have reached Level One.

Level Two is more cognitive. It involves judgments about feelings. If you are satisfied with your life, if you reflect on your pleasures and pains and feel that, overall, the balance is positive, you've reached Level Two. You are likely to report a general sense of satisfaction or wellbeing.

And Level Three? According to Nettle, you reach Level Three only when you feel like you are flourishing, fulfilling your life's potential. Level Three is about living the highest quality life.

What is that, exactly?

I'm tempted to paraphrase Louis Armstrong. Asked by an interviewer to define jazz, he replied "Man, if you gotta ask, you'll never know."

Clearly, however, a high-quality life is not synonymous with simply making a lot of money.

I'm not an idealist arguing that money doesn't matter. It does.

Money determines your neighborhood and the house your kids grow up in. It determines whether they go to college and where. It can decide whether you get a good doctor or an amazing doctor. If you need a lawyer, it determines whether you get an ambulance chaser or the best defense attorney money can buy. It provides freedom, security, and peace of mind.

In short, money matters. But it doesn't buy genuine love or friendship. It won't solve your problems, end your worries, fix your marriage, make you "a success," or even make you more charitable. People without money often imagine it will do all these things. It won't.

That's because money doesn't change you. It magnifies you, making it clear to everyone who you really are. In the end, you are who you are because of the choices you make, not the amount of money you have.

As author and TV personality Larry Winget says, "If Paris, Britney and Lindsey weren't rich, they would still be crashing cars and acting stupid at Wal-Mart instead of on Rodeo Drive. You just wouldn't know about it. . . . Money doesn't make you stupid. It just gets your picture taken more often."

Some folks might wonder what creates high-level satisfaction, if not the blessings that money can buy.

In his book *EconoPower: How a New Generation of Scientists is Transforming the World,* my friend and colleague Mark Skousen provides a pretty good answer. The four elements of happiness, he says, are:

1. Rewarding and honest employment
2. Recreation
3. Love and friendship
4. Spiritual development

Notice that number 1 is a pretty tough hurdle for retirees, and helps explain why so many slip into depression after leaving the workforce.

Notice, too, that none of the four elements requires money. (Though I'll concede that if you're broke, your recreation is more likely to be hiking, swimming, or reading than yachting and racing thoroughbreds.)

Perhaps the best description of Level Three happiness was put forward by Aristotle a few thousand years ago in the *Nicomachean Ethics.*

The Greek philosopher argued that we seek happiness in all the wrong places. We chase pleasure, excitement, and profit. Not that these things aren't enjoyable. But they don't create lasting contentment, because they are not what matters most.

What matters most, says Aristotle, is realizing your potential, living up to your values, and following your conscience. It's these things that create "the good life." It's these virtues that lead to a deep and abiding sense of happiness (what Nettle calls Level Three).

Following the dictates of conscience is never easy, of course. In many ways we will fall short. Still, it's better to fail at what is worth pursuing than to succeed at what is not.

Where is your conscience leading you today? Chances are you already know.

As General Norman Schwartzkopf famously said, "The truth of the matter is you always know the right thing to do. The hard part is doing it." ∎

THE GREAT MYSTERY

There has been a lot of fear and uncertainty in the financial markets recently.

We're struggling with the worst credit crisis since the 1930s. The S&P 500 has plunged. *Investor's Business Daily* reports that over 90 percent of all stock and bond mutual funds lost money last year.

Millions of investors have rushed into Treasuries. Many will stay there until they find someone who can tell them when the coast is clear again.

Unfortunately, that person doesn't exist.

I was an investment advisor and portfolio manager for many years. I've been a financial writer for the past eight. I don't know what the market is going to do in the short term. And I'm not the least bit reluctant to admit it. Because no one else knows either.

However, there are plenty of people on Wall Street—and in the financial media—who make a good living pretending to know or, in some cases, deluding themselves that they really *do* know.

This is a deadly mindset. (Pride isn't one of the seven deadly sins for nothing.)

Anyone can make a good market call. But no one can accurately predict the economy, interest rates, inflation, the value of the dollar, or the financial markets.

Count yourself a sophisticated investor the day you finally say to yourself, "Since no one can tell me with any consistency what lies just ahead for the economy and the stock market, how should I run my money?"

This inability to know what the future holds drives many investors to distraction. (Or, in some cases, the poor house.) But, to a great extent, markets are always inscrutable.

As Jason Zweig recently wrote in the *Wall Street Journal,* "Uncertainty is all investors ever have gotten, or ever will get, from the moment barley and sesame began trading in ancient Mesopotamia to the last trade that will ever take place on Planet Earth. If tomorrow were ever knowable with absolute certainty, who would take the other side of the trade today? . . . The only true certainty is surprise."

When I began studying the world's great investors more than two decades ago, I soon discovered that they used many different investment strategies. But they all approached the market with a deep sense of humility.

Benjamin Graham, the father of value investing, said, "If I have noticed anything over these 60 years on Wall Street, it is that people do not succeed in forecasting what is going to happen to the stock market."

Warren Buffett, the world's richest man and chairman of Berkshire Hathaway, once told shareholders, "We've long felt that the only value of stock forecasters is to make fortune tellers look good. Even now, Charlie [Munger] and I continue to believe that short-term market forecasts are poison and should be kept locked up in a safe place, away from children and also from grown-ups who behave in the market like children."

In his book *One Up On Wall Street,* Peter Lynch, the best mutual fund manager of all time, wrote, "Thousands of experts study overbought indicators, oversold indicators, head-and-shoulder patterns, put-call ratios, the Fed's policy on money supply, foreign investment, the movement of the constellations through the heavens, and the moss on oak trees, and they can't predict the markets with any useful consistency, any more than the gizzard squeezers could tell the Roman emperors when the Huns would attack."

These men understood that humility is essential to investment success—as it is to so much else in our lives.

Humility doesn't mean selling yourself short or not exercising your talents to the fullest. It means making an honest appraisal of the limited knowledge, experience, and understanding that we all bring to life.

It means having a realistic perspective, understanding that—whatever our particular talents—we are not the center of the universe. "We are all worms," Winston Churchill remarked. "But I do believe I am a glow-worm."

Humility is becoming. It wears well. Truly confident individuals don't need to brag or boast. It's much more attractive for people to discover your many charms on their own.

Secure individuals don't lord their status over others. Even if you are a truly one-in-a-million kind of guy, in a world of six billion people that means there are thousands more just like you.

A companionable friend or dinner guest knows better topics of conversation than himself. "There are two types of people in this world," observed Frederick L. Collins. "Those who come into the room and say, 'Well, here I am!' and those who come in and say, 'Ah, there you are!'"

Could anyone really prefer spending time with the former?

A modest attitude also demonstrates maturity. "Let us be humble," said Jawaharlal Nehru. "Let us think that the truth may not perhaps be entirely with us."

Live long enough and you're likely to learn that life is one long lesson in humility. Things don't always turn out like we planned . . . or even how we could have imagined.

Our happiness is determined, in large part, by how we handle these inevitable surprises. Because uncertainty will always be with us. Perhaps that is why Pulitzer Prize–winning columnist George Will once described his idea of heaven as "infinite knowing."

Recognizing the limits of our knowledge is invaluable, whether we're analyzing problems, figuring out relationships—or even puzzling over the big existential questions. Why are we here? Where did we come from? What's it all about?

Scientists, philosophers, and theologians have struggled with these for thousands of years. And still wrestle with them today.

As Nobel Prize–winning particle physicist Leon Lederman wryly observed, the universe is the answer. What we still don't know is the question.

This humble attitude has been embraced by great minds throughout history, from Aristotle to Newton to Einstein to Gandhi.

As Sioux Indian chief Ota Kte observed a century ago, "After all the great religions have been preached and expounded, or have been revealed by brilliant scholars, or have been written in books and embellished in fine language with fine covers, man—all man—is still confronted with *the Great Mystery.*" ■

THE DECENT
DRAPERY OF LIFE

During tough times, the nation's Presidential contest follows a familiar plot.

The candidate out of office invariably raises the age-old question, "Are you better off now than you were four years ago?"

When politicians pose this question, we know they are asking us to do a quick economic calculation. Is your salary higher? Is your home worth more? Is your 401(k) rising in value?

Given the bruised condition of the U.S. economy, housing market, and stock market, millions of Americans recently responded with an emphatic "no"—and a few overripe tomatoes.

Politics aside, though, there is a problem with turning this "better-off" question into a monetary equation. It neglects what Edmund Burke called "the decent drapery of life."

You may not be earning more than you were four years ago. Your home or your stock portfolio may be worth less. But is that really how we should really determine whether we are better off?

Maybe you fell in love over the last four years. Maybe you took up fly fishing. Maybe you moved to an exciting new city. (I did.) Maybe you spent the last four years honoring your profession, learning more about it, helping more people than ever before.

Economic statistics are fine as far as they go. But they don't go far in measuring a life well lived.

It can't just be about the grim determination to get and have more. As President Calvin Coolidge said, "No person was ever honored for what he received. Honor has been the reward for what he gave."

Columnist Peggy Noonan agrees. She writes,

> In a way, the world is a great liar. It shows you it worships and admires money, but at the end of the day it doesn't, not really. The world admires, and wants to hold on to, and not lose, goodness. It admires virtue. At the end it gives its greatest tributes to generosity, honesty, courage, mercy, talents well used, talents that, brought into the world, make it better. That's what it really admires. That's what we talk about in eulogies, because that's what's important. We don't say, "The thing about Joe was that he was rich." We say, if we can, "The thing about Joe was he took care of people."

It doesn't hurt to remember this. Because the one undeniable fact about the last four years is that you now have four less of them left.

So maybe the important thing is not to make more, have more, or spend more. Maybe the important thing is to slow down and appreciate small things, ordinary things: The first frost. The town clock. The curl on your grandson's forehead.

At 79, for instance, my Dad has suddenly become an avid birder. What a surprise. When I was growing up, his free time was all about golfing, coaching Little League games, or watching major league sports. He didn't own a pair of binoculars. And he certainly couldn't tell you the difference between a tufted titmouse and a yellow-bellied sapsucker.

When we're young, of course, we're going to live forever. There isn't time to notice a lot of things. We have places to go, things to do.

"We get to think of life as an inexhaustible well," wrote Paul Bowles near the end of his life. "Yet everything happens only a certain number of times, and a very small number, really. How many more times will you remember a certain afternoon of your childhood, some afternoon that's so deeply a part of your being that you can't even conceive of your life without it? Perhaps four or five times more, perhaps not even that. How many more times will you watch the full moon rise? Perhaps twenty."

Rushing from one appointment to the next, we use up our time, putting off the non-urgent, the unessential.

But in the second half—and no one knows when we reach that point exactly—life takes on a special poignancy precisely because our time is limited. It becomes richer and more meaningful *because of it.*

It becomes more important than ever to spend time with the people we love, to create those opportunities—and to savor them.

Are you better off than you were four years ago? Only you can determine what the question even means. But the answer shouldn't require a calculator.

"Enjoy life, it's ungrateful not to," Ronald Reagan once remarked.

They understand this in Scotland. When I lived in St. Andrews several years ago, the locals would often clink my glass, give a wink, and announce in that distinct Scottish brogue:

"Be happy while you're living, for you're a long time dead." ∎

THE DIFFERENCE BETWEEN *GETTING* RICH AND *BEING* RICH

A few years ago, Donald Trump wrote a book titled *How to Get Rich.* Ho-hum.

Far superior, in my view, is *How to Be Rich* by J. Paul Getty, originally published in 1965.

Trump focuses almost exclusively on making money. Getty—the world's first billionaire—is more concerned with wealth as a way of life.

"After all," he writes, "'richness' is at least as much a matter of character, of philosophy, of outlook and attitude, as it is of money. The 'millionaire mentality' is not—and in this day and age, cannot be—merely an accumulative mentality. The able, ambitious man who strives for success must understand that the term 'rich' has infinite shadings of meaning."

Getty's consuming passion, aside from building a considerable fortune in the oil business, was art. Throughout his life, he collected hundreds of paintings, sculptures, tapestries, and fine antiques. (Many of them are now on display at the J. Paul Getty Museum in Los Angeles.) He was a great believer in the enriching qualities of art. And he viewed with disdain the lowbrow culture of our time, often referring to his fellow men as "educated barbarians."

"Entirely too many Americans insist that they can see no reason for developing any cultural interests or appreciation of the arts. Some say they 'haven't time' for cultural pursuits. Yet, week after week, they will spend dozens of hours at country clubs, loafing here or there, or slumped in easy chairs in their homes staring blankly at the vulgar banalities that flash across the screens of their television sets."

(Bear in mind, this was written 40 years before the advent of "Reality TV.")

"Americans must realize that an understanding and appreciation of literature, drama, art, music—in short, of culture—will give them a broader, better foundation in life, and will enable them to enjoy life more fully. It will provide them with better balance and perspective, with interests that are pleasing to the senses and inwardly gratifying."

Personally, I've always had an amateur's interest in the arts. But lately I've been stretching out a bit, experiencing things I wouldn't usually bother with. In the process, I've made a few surprising discoveries.

Last year, for instance, a friend and I ventured out one night in a pouring rainstorm to hear a concert sponsored by a local art gallery. It was Le Trio Joubran, three oud players (and a percussionist) from Palestine. It was highly improvised Middle Eastern music, definitely not the kind of thing you'd hear at The House of Blues. It was pretty exotic—and exceptionally good.

The next week I dropped in on the Kerouac Festival at a local community college to hear a recital by Billy Collins, the nation's Poet Laureate from 2001 to 2003. Some readers may spontaneously recoil at the thought of listening to 90 minutes of poetry, with no place to run. But settle down.

Collins writes in a lucid, plain-spoken style that even lay readers can appreciate. And he finds poetry in the most mundane aspects of everyday life. For example:

Dharma

The way the dog trots out the front door
every morning

without a hat or an umbrella,
without any money
or the keys to her doghouse
never fails to fill the saucer of my heart
with milky admiration.
Who provides a finer example
of a life without encumbrance—
Thoreau in his curtainless hut
with a single plate, a single spoon?
Gandhi with his staff and his holy diapers?
Off she goes into the material world
with nothing but her brown coat
and her modest blue collar,
following only her wet nose,
the twin portals of her steady breathing,
followed only by the plume of her tail.
If only she did not shove the cat aside
every morning
and eat all his food
what a model of self-containment she
would be,
what a paragon of earthly detachment.
If only she were not so eager
for a rub behind the ears,
so acrobatic in her welcomes,
if only I were not her god.

Okay, this is not "Death Be Not Proud," but so what? When was the last time you heard an audience laughing and enthusiastically applauding through a poetry recital?

J. Paul Getty was onto something—the idea of *being* rich, not just having riches. Sure, exposing yourself to art is just one aspect of enriching your life, but an important one. As the German writer Johann Wolfgang von Goethe wrote several hundred years ago, "One ought, every day at least, to hear a little song, read a good poem, see a fine picture, and if it were possible, to speak a few reasonable words."

Take a few minutes to peruse the Weekend section of your local paper and I'll bet you'll find a concert, a gallery, a play—something—new to appreciate. And to share.

In the end, not everyone among us will get rich. But we each have the opportunity to *be* rich.   ■

The Key to Perfect Freedom

Not long ago, I was playing golf with a friend who is an attorney. Between shots he began telling me how much he detested his job.

"Why?" I asked.

"You have to understand my business," he said with a huff. "My day basically consists of writing nasty letters on behalf of my clients. Then we get nasty letters back. This goes on for a few weeks until my clients realize how many billable hours they've run up. Then *they* start getting nasty with me. The whole business," he said with a shake of his head, "is kind of *nasty*."

"Why don't you do something else?" I asked.

From the look on his face, you would have thought I suggested he stop breathing.

"Do something else?" he said. "You don't understand. I live in a *big* house. I have two *big* cars. My wife and I take *big* trips. She runs up *big* bills. What else am I gonna do?"

"I don't know," I said. "But it all sounds like a big *mistake* to me."

The sad part is my buddy is a bright, talented guy. He's giving up a lot. With his experience and law degree, there are plenty of other things he could do.

But he doesn't believe that's realistic. Why? Because, like most of us, he can't tolerate the thought of a temporary loss of status and income. Unfortunately, that's usually the price of admission.

As the psychologist Laurence G. Boldt once wrote, "The life you spend doing what you love is a different life indeed from putting your life out for hire to the highest bidder. The only way you can say it makes no difference is to say life makes no difference."

These words hit me between the eyes when I first read them eight years ago. At the time I had spent sixteen years working on Wall Street. My job paid well, but I had grown increasingly bored with what I was doing.

I loved analyzing the market, but I'd grown tired of having the same repetitive conversations with my clients about their accounts every day.

So I left to write about the financial markets, instead.

My co-workers thought I had lost my mind. "Nobody gets to the point where he has all these clients, all these assets, and all this income and then just walks away," one colleague told me, incredulous. "If you leave, you're really going to regret it."

But I haven't. Not for one minute. If anything, I wish I'd done it sooner. Joseph Campbell was right: Follow your bliss.

"If you follow your bliss," he wrote, "you put yourself on a kind of track, which has been there all the while waiting for you, and the life that you ought to be living is the one you are living . . . I think the person who takes a job in order to live—that is to say, just for the money—has turned himself into a slave."

That sounds harsh, I know. After all, we all have commitments and responsibilities. But that doesn't mean change isn't possible. It hurts to spend your days doing something that is not really suited to your talents, especially when you know you could be doing far more than you are.

Work you enjoy is invigorating. You're expressing yourself, making an impact.

As the British historian and philosopher R. G. Collingwood said, "Perfect freedom is reserved for the man who lives by his own work and in that work does what he wants to do."

Too many of us approach the job market thinking of nothing more than money, security, and benefits. I'm not saying these things aren't important. They are. None of us would survive long without them.

But for a true sense of fulfillment, there has to be more than just money and security. (Just as there has to be more to retirement than golf and television.) It's tough to feel genuinely satisfied without expressing your abilities, even if your primary talent is raising happy, productive kids.

As George Bernard Shaw said:

> This is the true joy in life, the being used for a purpose recognized by yourself as a mighty one; the being thoroughly worn out before you are thrown on the scrap heap; the being a force of nature instead of a feverish selfish little clod of ailments and grievances complaining that the world will not devote itself to making you happy.

Some may call Shaw an idealist, a dreamer. Perhaps. But life is not a practice round. This is it.

You can work a job. You can pursue a career. Or you can choose a vocation.

The choice is yours. ■

THE SECRET OF INSPIRATIONAL LEADERSHIP

When speaking at investment conferences, I try to emphasize the importance of "quality of management" when evaluating public companies.

What would Microsoft have become without Bill Gates? Apple without Steve Jobs? Or Berkshire Hathaway without Warren Buffett? It's hard to imagine.

On the flip side, ten years ago WorldCom had the most impressive array of telecommunications assets on the planet. But with Bernie Ebbers at the helm, it didn't matter. He drove the company right into bankruptcy.

Today Ebbers is serving 25 years at the Oakdale Federal Correctional Complex for orchestrating the biggest corporate fraud in U.S. history. (And I need hardly remind you what chieftains Ken Lay and Jeff Skilling did for Enron employees and shareholders.)

In the business world, physical assets are essential. Patents and trademarks are invaluable. Positive cash flow is wonderful. But, at the very heart of things, every organization is a team of people. And just as a winning sports franchise requires a great coach, every organization needs an inspiring leader. Because if the team isn't rowing in the same direction—the right direction—you won't get far.

I was reminded of this last year while attending a fundraising event for the American Cancer Society at the Royal Pacific Resort in Orlando. The keynote speaker was one of America's all-time great football coaches Lou Holtz.

Holtz is not just a multiple winner of "Coach of the Year" honors. He is the only coach in NCAA history to lead six different programs to bowl games. And the only coach to have four different teams reach final top 20 rankings.

Throughout his career, Holtz earned a reputation for both developing winning teams and quickly rebuilding broken ones. He has written five books on leadership. He claims he is the only man in America who has written more books than he has read.

Don't let him fool you. Lou Holtz is a living example of inspirational leadership. I hadn't intended to take notes, but a minute and a half into his talk I was scouring the table for a cocktail napkin.

"Leadership begins with recognizing that everybody needs four things," said Holtz, "something to do, someone to love, something to hope for, and something to believe in. Strategic plans don't excite anybody. Dreams excite people . . . And every employee, every team member, wants to know the same thing: Do you really care about me? Every successful organization shows its people they genuinely matter."

You may not coach a university football team or run a Fortune 500 company. But I'll bet you are in a position to provide inspirational leadership. How? First, by setting an example. Second, by letting the people around you know how important they are.

In a piece entitled "Godly Work" in the April 23, 2007 issue of *Forbes,* columnist Rich Karlgaard related a story he was told by Nancy Ortberg, an emergency room nurse who was finishing up work one night before heading home.

> "The doctor with whom I was working was debriefing a new doctor, who had done a very respectable, competent job, telling him what he'd done well and what he could have done differently.
>
> "Then he put his hand on the young doctor's shoulder and said, 'When you finished, did you notice the young man from

housekeeping who came in to clean the room?' There was a completely blank look on the young doctor's face.

"The older doctor said, 'His name is Carlos. He's been here for three years. He does a fabulous job. When he comes in he gets the room turned around so fast that you and I can get our next patients in quickly. His wife's name is Maria. They have four children.' Then he named each of the four children and gave each child's age.

"The older doctor went on to say, 'He lives in a rented house about three blocks from here, in Santa Ana. They've been up from Mexico for about five years. His name is Carlos,' he repeated. Then he said, 'Next week I would like you to tell me something about Carlos that I don't already know. Okay? Now, let's go check on the rest of the patients.'"

Ortberg recalls: "I remember standing there writing my nursing notes—stunned—and thinking, I have just witnessed breathtaking leadership."

Fostering mutual respect among colleagues is perhaps the most important ingredient for building and sustaining a healthy organization. It is people who matter most.

Yes, business will always be about meeting the deadline, closing the deal, finishing the project, and growing the business. But if your work life is nothing more than the single-minded pursuit of wealth, recognition, and accomplishment, you will wake up one day and find that *something* is still missing.

That's because true success is not just about achieving your dreams. It's about helping those around you reach theirs, too. ∎

■ ARE YOU ONE OF THE 4 PERCENT?

Several years ago, management consultant Dr. Gerald Kushel studied a representative sample of America's top executives. He found that only a small group—just 4 percent—rated themselves "very satisfied" with both their personal and professional lives.

I doubt many people were surprised to find that genuine contentment is a rare commodity in corporate boardrooms. We've all known hard-driving businessmen who ended up frustrated and burned-out, even if they met their professional and monetary goals. The executive who sacrifices his personal life to meet his business objectives is almost a proverb.

Yet this 4 percent maintained a remarkable sense of balance in their lives. Kushel found that "in addition to success in the marketplace, they manage to have extremely pleasing private lives, enduring and satisfying relationships with friends and family, and enjoy many quiet pleasures alone."

These executives had an uncanny knack for managing skillfully, delegating effectively, and reaching important business goals. But several important characteristics separated the 4 percent—the ones who were "very satisfied" with both their personal and professional lives—from the burned-out majority.

For starters, Kushel found that the 4 percent met none of these stereotypes:

- They take their work, the company, and their career very seriously.
- They ruin their family lives with their preoccupation with work.
- They operate under great stress.
- They are weighed down with multiple problems.
- They are real infighters.
- They have a strong need to control others, including both their peers and their subordinates.
- They stick to their guns when they're right.

It turns out that these qualities—which together represent a caricature of the harried business executive—were almost completely absent among those who were happiest with their lives both at home and at work.

Instead of seeing themselves as driven executives whose careers define their lives, Kushel discovered that the 4 percent have a sense of identity that goes far beyond their job description or even their family's definition of who they are.

Instead, they define themselves on their own terms. They see themselves as more than any one role at home or at the office. In fact, their identities are more generally drawn more from their values, their principles, their interests, or their philosophy of life.

It may not be unusual to find artists, academics, 9-to-5'ers, and assorted slackers with this point of view. But top executives?

Absolutely. One CEO of a national manufacturing company pled with Kushel, "Please don't let anyone know. If the people back at my company found out how lightly I take my job, they'd feel very much let down. They enjoy thinking of me as a workaholic. So sometimes when things go wrong, I feign worry and upset. They love it. Sometimes I act angry just to get my people moving. Acting angry can be productive, but really being angry usually makes very little sense. Deep down, I never forget that there are many, many more important things in this world than making profits."

Men and women with a heightened sense of self found it easier to achieve their objectives and accept occasional setbacks—even serious ones—with relative equanimity.

The 4 percent took responsibility for the circumstances in their lives. They virtually never saw their problems as the result of their spouses, their colleagues, their children, bad luck, or "the breaks." Rather, they consistently went out of their way to place the responsibility for unhappy outcomes on their own shoulders.

Acknowledging that we are largely responsible for the circumstances in our lives creates the power to change them.

Moreover, Kushel's survey reveals that those who want nothing more than money, power, and prestige are often frustrated by their inability to achieve it. Why? Because they want it so badly that they cramp their style, turn off potential allies, and inadvertently undo their own efforts. Those who put money and status in perspective, on the other hand, often achieved material success with relative ease.

I think the 4 percent are onto something here . . .

Conventional wisdom says that to get everything you want, it's often a matter of trying harder and "wanting it more." Kushel discovered just the opposite: Success at home and at work is more likely the result of putting yourself and your objectives in perspective . . . and, ironically, wanting it less. ∎

FINDING MEANING IN THE SECOND HALF OF LIFE

It is an ironic fact of modern life. We in the materially prosperous West are living the most successful and outwardly comfortable lives of any people in history.

Yet according to the National Library of Medicine, nearly 8 percent of U.S. adults—over 20 million people—are suffering from depression. Adjusting for population growth, depression is 10 times as prevalent today as it was 50 years ago.

No wonder the United States has been dubbed "Prozac Nation." According to the American Mental Health Alliance, we spend over $86 billion a year on antidepressants. (Insert low whistle here.)

Much of today's psychotherapy, unfortunately, is little more than a pharmacological crapshoot. Doctors prescribe a pill and if that doesn't work, well . . . heck, let's try another one. (Insurance providers actually prefer this approach, incidentally, because it's cheaper than therapy.) Yet studies show that roughly one-third of patients fail to respond to any kind of drug treatment.

Is it possible that some of these patients have a problem that a prescription—or even traditional therapy—can't solve?

Before you assume that I'll be joining Tom Cruise for an afternoon in La-La Land, hear me out . . .

Psychologists believe that roughly a quarter of Americans with symptoms of depression suffer from a chemical imbalance that, like diabetes, is most effectively treated with medication.

Others are experiencing a kind of reactive depression that is triggered by a serious reversal of some kind, an unexpected layoff, for example, or the sudden loss of a loved one. This form of depression can be severe but ordinarily fades with time.

Yet, according to Dr. James Hollis of the C. J. Jung Educational Center in Houston, millions more suffer from a chronic melancholy that emanates from an entirely different source: a lack of meaning in their lives.

This problem is particularly acute in retirement. In the workforce we are accustomed to having a place to be and a time to be there, with deadlines and projects to complete. In many ways, we draw our identity from our work.

So it can be a shock if retirement arrives and we discover that the days of rest and relaxation we so eagerly anticipated are instead boring or tedious.

Of course, you don't have to retire to experience a profound ennui. Millions of workers search in vain for meaning and fulfillment, too.

Many of them are haunted by the vague notion that something is missing in their lives. Often they can't put their finger on it. But it gnaws at them, creating fear, anxiety, and, in some cases, depression.

In his memoir *Memories, Dreams, Reflections,* pioneering psychologist Carl Jung writes, "I have frequently seen people become neurotic when they content themselves with inadequate or wrong answers to the questions of life. They seek position, marriage, reputation, outward success or money, and remain unhappy and neurotic even when they have attained what they were seeking. Such people are usually contained within too narrow a spiritual horizon. Their life has not sufficient meaning."

But if meaning is missing, where can it be found? Some find the answer in their religious traditions. Others discover it by studying the world's wisdom literature, the great writings by history's wisest souls. Still others are fortunate enough to see it modeled by a parent, friend, or teacher, someone who is not merely living up to someone else's expectations but is instead busy living "an authentic life."

These men and women are too rare. And when they appear, society tends to label them eccentric. As the poet T. S. Eliot observed, in a world of fugitives, the person who is headed in the right direction will appear to be running away.

Ironically, it is popular culture itself that sends many people down the wrong path, bombarding them with dubious notions of satisfaction and success.

It's tragic when someone sacrifices years of his life, his friendships, his family—sometimes even his health—pursuing goals that are ultimately unfulfilling. Mythologist Joseph Campbell once quipped that midlife is when you reach the top of the ladder and find it's leaning against the wrong wall.

That's why it cannot be said too often: Money. Possessions. Luxury. These are not the hallmarks of a life well lived. At best, they are merely by-products.

"Despite the blandishments of popular culture, the goal of life is not happiness but meaning," writes Dr. James Hollis, author of *Finding Meaning In the Second Half of Life.*

To determine whether you're on the right track, he suggests you ask yourself a simple question: "Does the path I'm on enlarge me or diminish me?" Your answer, he says, should be immediate and instinctive.

Yes, we're all busy. But can we possibly be too busy to get our priorities straight? After all, only you can determine what is most important in your life, whether you're working, retired, or somewhere in between. You get to decide—and pursue—what's most important.

Living an authentic life is not always easy. The poet e. e. cummings said, "To be nobody but yourself in a world which is doing its best, night and day, to make you everybody else means to fight the hardest battle which any human being can fight; and never stop fighting."

So expect conflicts and hurdles. Setbacks, too. Finding creative solutions to these challenges fuels the mind with positive energy. It gives you the opportunity to show yourself—and those around you—how much you really want it.

It gives your life meaning, too. As Carl Jung observed, "Meaning makes a great many things endurable—perhaps everything." ∎

The Value of Being Utterly, Gloriously Wrong

When I started managing client monies back in the mid-1980s, I was as green as a Granny Smith apple.

Although I was confident I knew what I was doing, I ended up getting my head handed to me in the market. And not just once.

My investment strategy was a completely blinkered market-timing approach. And while I believed in it heart and soul at the time, it had little chance of success. (Pity my early clients.) Things never got better until the day I recognized that fact.

No one relishes the idea of being utterly and profoundly wrong. But discovering we *are* can be one of life's most rewarding experiences.

For reasons of pride, ego, hubris, or fear, however, we have trouble accepting this. That means we miss some of the best lessons life has to offer.

After all, when you admit you're wrong, all you're essentially saying is that you know more today than you did yesterday.

Yet studies show that we glom onto ideas early and resist letting them go. Psychologists call it "confirmation bias." That is, we seek evidence that confirms our beliefs and ignore or reinterpret evidence that refutes them.

It's easy to see how. We all gravitate toward like-minded souls, listen primarily to those who share our opinions, and read books and articles by writers who confirm our point of view.

But the narrower our sources of information, the more error-prone our thinking becomes. Our primary exercise becomes jumping to conclusions.

In a 1989 study, for example, psychologist Deanna Kuhn found that when subjects were exposed to evidence inconsistent with a theory they preferred, they failed to notice it. When they did recognize the contradictory evidence, they simply reinterpreted it in favor of their preconceived belief.

In a related study, *Scientific American* columnist Michael Shermer writes that "Kuhn played an audio recording of an actual murder trial and discovered that instead of evaluating the evidence first and then coming to a conclusion, most subjects concocted a narrative in their mind about what happened, made a decision of guilt or innocence, then riffled through the evidence and picked out what most closely fit the story."

Knowing this, is it terribly surprising that so far more than 200 death-row inmates in the United States have been exonerated by DNA evidence? (Maybe Woody Allen wasn't kidding when he said he'd hate to leave his fate in the hands of twelve people who weren't smart enough to get out of jury duty.)

In truth, by looking at the evidence with an open mind we have nothing to lose but our ignorance. And when our views *are* correct we solidify them, making them stronger.

In his book *Confessions of a Philosopher,* Bryan Magee writes that he became a skilled debater by identifying his opponent's weak points and then bringing concentrated fire to bear on them, a tactic used by successful polemicists since ancient times.

Yet he was blown away when he discovered that philosopher Karl Popper did just the opposite:

> He sought out his opponent's case at its strongest and attacked that. Indeed, he would improve it, if he possibly could, before

attacking it. . . . He would remove avoidable contradictions or weaknesses, close loopholes, pass over minor deficiencies, let his opponent's case have the benefit of every possible doubt, and reformulate the most appealing parts of it in the most rigorous, powerful and effective arguments he could find—and then direct his onslaught against it. The outcome, when successful, was devastating. At the end there would be nothing left to say in favor of the opposing case except for tributes and concessions that Popper himself had already made.

It must have been thrilling to witness. Yet no one reaches this level of understanding without taking the time to thoroughly investigate an opposing view rather than dismissing it out of hand. It takes time to weigh the evidence, consider it, and allow for the possibility that we could be mistaken. This is something that most of us—if we're honest with ourselves—are reluctant to do.

When you bring an open mind to a conflict, one of three things will happen. You'll strengthen your existing convictions. You'll become more sympathetic to the opposing view. Or you'll end up smarter today than you were yesterday—and get a lesson in humility in the bargain.

That's why you should never lose your temper in an argument. If you're right, you don't need to. If you're wrong, you can't afford to.

As the French Enlightenment professor Voltaire said, "Doubt is not a pleasant condition, but certainty is an absurd one." ■

ADVICE FROM A
2000-YEAR-OLD SLAVE

Standing in line at the register the other day, I couldn't help overhearing the woman on her cell phone in front of me.

Her mother had abused her. Her employer didn't appreciate her. Her husband didn't understand her. Her kids disrespected her. By the time she was done, I could have sworn I heard the sun was too bright outside and the birds were singing too loud.

Some things never change . . .

If a citizen of ancient Greece or Rome were magically transported into the modern era, he would be astounded by the current state of agriculture, transportation, housing, medicine, architecture, technology, and living standards.

But humanity itself would offer few surprises. We remain the same flawed human beings we always were, struggling with the same deadly sins our ancestors wrestled with millennia ago.

That is why ancient philosophers still speak to us—if we listen. The wisdom of the classical world transcends place and time.

The Stoic philosophy, for example, dominated the ancient world for nearly 600 years, beginning in the late 4th century B.C.E.

Stoics believed that reason was supreme. Tranquility is only achieved, they taught, by suppressing irrational emotions—like regrets about the past—and accepting life's unavoidable disappointments and setbacks.

One of the great exponents of Stoicism was a slave named Epictetus, born around 55 C.E. in the eastern outreaches of the Roman Empire.

Epictetus had few advantages in life. Aside from being born into slavery, he was crippled. And he was poor, living a simple life in a small hut with no possessions.

Yet he became one of the leading thinkers of his age. When Epictetus was freed from slavery—we still don't know how—he set up a philosophical school on the northwest coast of Greece, spending his days lecturing on how to live with greater dignity and tranquility.

As his reputation for wisdom grew, people flocked to hear him. One of his most distinguished students was the young Marcus Aurelius Antonius, who eventually became ruler of the Roman Empire.

Epictetus was not one for airy theories. In his view, the job of philosophy is to help ordinary people deal with the challenges of everyday life. And his words, captured in *The Art of Living,* are as wise today as when he spoke them nearly 2,000 years ago:

Keep your attention focused entirely on what is truly your own concern, and be clear that what belongs to others is their business and none of yours.

One of the clearest marks of the moral life is right speech. . . . Glib talk disrespects others. Breezy self-disclosure disrespects yourself. . . . If need be, be mostly silent or speak sparingly.

Let the quality of your deeds speak on your behalf. We can't control the impressions others form about us, and the effort to do so only debases our character. So, if anyone should tell you that a particular person has spoken critically of you, don't bother with excuses or defenses. Just smile and reply, "I guess that person doesn't know about all my other faults. Otherwise, he wouldn't have mentioned only these."

Now is the time to get serious about living your ideals. Once you have determined the spiritual principles you wish to exemplify, abide by these rules as if they were laws.

Epictetus had a deep understanding of human beings, of society . . . and of life. But he understood death, too.

> I must die. If the time is now, I'm ready. . . . How will I die? Like a man who gives up what belongs to another. . . . A good death can only come from a good life.

Epictetus argued that our prime motivation should be inner achievements, not outer ones. The right attitudes and values allow you to flourish no matter what the external world throws at you. Inner achievement lays the foundation for peace, tranquility, and personal freedom. And so he taught that true success comes from refocusing ourselves within:

> We cannot choose our external circumstances, but we can always choose how to respond to them.

> If someone irritates you, it is only your own response that is irritating you. Therefore, when anyone seems to be provoking you, remember that it is only your judgment of the incident that provokes you.

> Those who are dedicated to a life of wisdom understand that the impulse to blame something or someone is foolishness, that there is nothing to be gained in blaming, whether it be others or oneself.

> If anyone is unhappy, remember that his unhappiness is his own fault. . . . Nothing else is the cause of anxiety or loss of tranquility except our own opinion.

> He is wise who doesn't grieve for the things he doesn't have, but rejoices for the things he does have.

> Fortify yourself with contentment, for it is an impregnable fortress.

Whether you are a street sweeper or a CEO, Epictetus insists that your main job in life—your most important task—is improving yourself. Yet, always the realist, he emphasized moral progress over moral *perfection*.

Today Epictetus is widely recognized as the world's first philosopher of personal freedom. Its attainment, he insisted, is the result of mastering our thoughts, yielding to the inevitable, pursuing virtue rather than wealth, and diverting our attention from constant desire, yearning and attachment.

In a modern translation of *The Art of Living,* philosophical writer Sharon Lebell observes that, "His was a moral teaching stripped of sentimentality, piousness, and metaphysical mumbojumbo. What remains is the West's first and best primer for living the best possible life."

Ironic, isn't it? A man born into slavery was among the first to show us the path to personal liberation.

"Anyone is free who lives as he wishes to live," said Epictetus. "And no one is free who is not master of himself." ∎

THE HARDEST VICTORY

I recently spoke at a VIP Traders Conference in New York City.

Investors gather at these events to discuss various approaches to the stock market. I remind them, however, that success will not come from adopting a particular trading technique or even from buying the "right" investments.

No, their results will depend on the same thing that determines our success in virtually everything we do: self-discipline.

Investing is not rocket science. All you need is a proven approach, realistic expectations, and the discipline to follow through.

As with most things in life, easier said than done.

Take dieting, for example. It is estimated that Americans spend up to $6 billion annually on dieting aids. But let's be honest with ourselves. Dieting is not about Atkins, South Beach, Jenny Craig, or NutriSystem. Nor is it about cholesterol, carbs, sugars, or fat grams.

It's about math. Every day of your life you either take in more calories than you burn or burn more calories than you take in. (Glance in the direction of your belt buckle to see your running total.)

You already know which foods are good for you and which ones aren't. No one needs to tell you "breakfast of fruit and yogurt—good. Donuts and coffee—bad." "Tuna fish and salad for lunch—good. Whopper and fries—bad." Come on. Losing weight is about nothing more than committing to a healthy diet and regular exercise.

I happen to be an expert on this subject, incidentally. Over the past two years I've been trying to lose ten pounds, and, so far, all I've lost is two years.

I don't kid myself that my diet and exercise program "hasn't worked." *I* haven't worked. I haven't gotten off my fat duff often enough—and rarely passed on that fresh slice of New York cheese-cake slathered with raspberry sauce.

We can blame circumstances all we want. In our hearts, we know that lack of genuine commitment is the real reason for most of our unmet goals, whether in academics, athletics, career advancement, wealth building, you name it. Fortunately, this is something we can change.

"Self-discipline is the foundation of freedom," writes Matthew Kelly in *The Rhythm of Life*. "It is the foundation of greatness, achievement, heroism, leadership, sanctity, and vibrant and flourishing communities and nations. . . . If you examine the lives of men and women who have achieved little or nothing with their lives, people who are miserable, mean and dispassionate, you will discover that it was not other people who destroyed their lives. Destruction always comes from within."

A satisfied life comes from meeting your most important objectives. And that means doing what needs to be done, without wasting time or energy worrying about whether you feel like it. As the Nike slogan insists, "Just do it."

"When we develop the habit of plunging in without whining, complaining or procrastinating, we are on our way to genuine freedom," observes author Laurence G. Boldt. "We may not want to face it in such stark terms, but the choice is self-discipline or dependency; boss yourself or be bossed."

Some folks imagine that making personal commitments and keeping them is a chore. It may feel that way at first. But, ultimately, it can be liberating. Wise men and women have understood this for centuries.

"Choose always the way that seems the best, however rough it may be; custom will soon render it easy and agreeable," proclaimed the Greek mathematician Pythagoras. "No man is free who cannot command himself."

The Roman philosopher Seneca concurred. "Let us train our minds to desire what the situation demands."

"I count him braver who overcomes his desires than him who conquers his enemies," said Aristotle. "The hardest victory is the victory over self."

Millions have the ambition to succeed—and the aptitude as well. Why do so few move ahead? Perhaps they imagine that since they can master the job, there is no need to master themselves.

Big mistake. Seldom are we able to govern events. More often we are challenged to govern ourselves.

As Siddhartha Gautama said 2,400 years ago: "Carpenters bend wood; fletchers bend arrows; wise men fashion themselves." ■

In Praise of Difficult Pleasures

Last year my brother Carter invited me to attend a performance of *King Lear* at the Blackfriars Playhouse in Staunton, VA.

The 300-seat playhouse is the only re-creation of the first indoor theater in the English-speaking world, the one William Shakespeare and his colleagues built on part of London's Blackfriars Monastery.

The resident company has received international acclaim for its performance of Shakespeare's works under their original staging conditions—a simple stage, without elaborate sets, with the audience sharing the same lights as the actors.

King Lear, of course, is Shakespeare's profound and timeless exploration of the meaning of life. And the performance that evening was exceptional, with the actors clearly relishing their roles. (Superior acting can often bring to life qualities that lie dormant on the page.)

I confess that I have not invested as much time as I'd like reading The Bard. But that's changing.

Like generations before me, I often complained that "Shakespeare was ruined for me in high school." You may have had the same experience.

Elizabethan English is a challenge for modern readers. And when we're young, it's too early for much of Shakespeare to resonate with us.

If you haven't experienced great triumphs, temptations, disappointments, love affairs, false friends, a broken heart, the corrupting influence of politics, or the pleasures and tribulations of parenthood, Shakespeare may cross your head at 30,000 feet.

Then, too, there is the way Shakespeare is often taught, especially the sonnets.

In his poem "Introduction to Poetry," former Poet Laureate Billy Collins writes that teachers often "tie the poem to a chair with rope and torture a confession out of it. / They begin beating it with a hose to find out what it really means."

If that sounds eerily reminiscent of your own introduction to Shakespeare, you may want to try again.

Why bother? One reason is that Shakespeare is the presiding genius of the English language. Another is the profound enjoyment you can receive tackling "difficult pleasures."

Shakespeare is a good example. The author of 38 plays, 154 sonnets, and many poems, he wrote the best poetry and prose in English.

He thought more comprehensively and originally than any writer before or since. No other playwright's works are performed more frequently. Only the Bible has been more widely translated. Shakespeare is rightly venerated.

If I'm approaching what George Bernard Shaw called "bardolatry," consider what Bill Bryson says in his biography *Shakespeare: The World as Stage*: "If we take the *Oxford Dictionary of Quotations* as our guide, then Shakespeare produced roughly one-tenth of all the most quotable utterances written or spoken in English since its inception—a clearly remarkable proportion."

Remarkable? That billions of people have spoken the language and a single individual is responsible for roughly 10 percent of the most quotable things ever said is almost beyond belief.

Shakespeare's influence is so pervasive that we walk around quoting him every day without even realizing it.

Just a small sampling of phrases originally found in Shakespeare's works include *flesh and blood, bated breath, tower of strength, foul play, foregone conclusion, good riddance, dead as a doornail, fool's paradise, heart of gold, Greek to me, fancy-free, devil incarnate, one fell swoop, for goodness' sake, vanish into thin air, play fast and loose, eaten me out of house and home, elbow room, go down the primrose path, in a pickle, budge an inch, cold comfort, household word, full circle, salad days, in my heart of hearts, in my mind's eye, laughing stock, love is blind, lie low, naked truth, neither rhyme nor reason, star-crossed lovers, pitched battle, pound of flesh, sea change, make short shrift, spotless reputation, set my teeth on edge, there's the rub, too much of a good thing, what the dickens,* and *wild goose chase.*

Despite these now-common phrases, you may have been turned off by Shakespeare in the past simply because you encountered so many unfamiliar words. If so, you're in good company. Many of them were unfamiliar to his audiences 400 years ago.

Indeed, during his productive peak he was coining new words at a rate of one *every two and a half lines.* (Scholars claim that Hamlet alone gave audiences nearly 600 words they had never heard before.)

In his biography, Bryson points out that "among the words first found in Shakespeare are *abstemious, antipathy, critical, frugal, dwindle, extract, horrid, vast, hereditary, excellent, eventful, barefaced, assassination, lonely, leapfrog, indistinguishable, well-read, zany,* and countless others (including *countless*)."

Of course, Shakespeare isn't considered one of the great creative geniuses just because he kept Noah Webster awake at night. He created utterly original and consistent voices for more than a hundred major characters and several hundred minor ones. In the process, he showed the world what it means to be human.

In *Shakespeare: The Invention of the Human,* Harold Bloom says, "Shakespeare's uncanny power in the rendering of personality is perhaps beyond explanation. Why do his personages seem so real to us, and how could he contrive that illusion so persuasively? . . . The plays remain the outward limit of human achievement: aesthetically, cognitively, in certain ways morally, even spiritually."

If you haven't read Shakespeare, there's still time to discover (or rediscover) him. And you should. As Henry David Thoreau advised, "Read the best books first, or you may not have a chance to read them at all."

Even if you initially find Shakespeare complex, obscure, or "not to your taste," keep plugging. There can be deep satisfaction in difficult pleasures. By their very nature, however, they require time and persistence.

If you offer a 6-year-old a choice between a hot dog or linguine with white clam sauce, for instance, she will invariably go for the frankfurter. No surprise here. A 6-year-old hasn't developed his palate.

Offer the average teenager a choice between a rap song or Ella Fitzgerald singing a selection from the Cole Porter songbook, and he'll prefer the tune where his subwoofer can be heard two blocks away.

Most of us understand why. (I went through my own "bad-haircut, loud-clothes, and god-awful music" phase.)

Yet as we reach middle age and beyond, our tastes generally mature. They become more refined. We give up comic books and pulp fiction for history and literature. We play bridge, gin, or poker rather than Crazy Eights or Old Maid. We may prefer a single malt scotch or glass of Sauvignon Blanc to a Budweiser (unless, of course, there's a game on).

In short, we begin to enjoy the challenge and mental exercise of more difficult pleasures. It's part of growing up, realizing your potential, and becoming who you are.

If you already prefer chess to checkers, the *New York Times* crossword puzzle to *People* magazine, or Sudoku to an in-flight Adam Sandler flick, we're probably in agreement here.

Aside from the sheer enjoyment of tackling more challenging pastimes, studies show that exercising your mental faculties helps prevent the onset of mild depression, dementia, and other mental disabilities.

So challenge yourself and get those brain cells moving. A few years from now you'll be the same person you are today, except for the experiences you have and the books you read.

Fortunately, there are plenty of great works out there. Few, however, are superior to Shakespeare. So pick up a recording of the sonnets, attend a play at your local theater, or rent Laurence Olivier's 1948 masterpiece *Hamlet*.

And don't feel like you have to tough it out. Cheat a little—as I often do before a performance—by picking up a copy of *Shakespeare Made Easy* or *Simply Shakespeare,* containing modern line-for-line translations beside the original text. Once you're familiar with the plot, the language won't be an obstacle to your enjoyment.

Spark Notes has even posted modern translations of nineteen major Shakespeare works—including the sonnets—online for free.

If you revisit Shakespeare and do find him too challenging to be pleasurable, back up and read Jane Austen, Oscar Wilde, or Mark Twain. Then try again. It will be time well spent.

As the Russian poet Joseph Alexandrovich Brodsky observed, "There are worse crimes than burning books. One of them is not reading them." ■

The True Gentleman

I've always enjoyed Oscar Wilde's comedy *An Ideal Husband*. But *New York Times* columnist Maureen Dowd is out to help women find the genuine item.

In a recent column, she shared the wisdom of Father Pat Connor, a 79-year-old Catholic priest with several decades of experience as a marriage counselor.

Too many women marry badly, he says, because infatuation trumps judgment. (I'm sure plenty of men have their own complaints, but today is Ladies' Day.)

Father Connor advises women not to marry a man who has no friends, who is controlling or irresponsible with money, who is overly attached to his mother, or who has no sense of humor. He lists so many qualities to avoid, in fact, that some women responded despairingly that he'd "eliminated everyone."

Not yet . . .

The column generated a hailstorm of letters to the editor, including one from a Ms. Susan Striker of Easton, CT. The twice-divorced woman offered that Father Connor had only scratched the surface. She warns women:

Never marry a man who yells at you in front of his friends.
Never marry a man who is more affectionate in public than in private.
Never marry a man who notices all of your faults but never notices his own.

Never marry a man whose first wife had to sue him for child
   support.
Never marry a man who corrects you in public.
Never marry a man who sends birthday cards to his ex-girlfriends.
Never marry a man who doesn't treat his dog nicely.
Never marry a man who is rude to waiters.
Never marry a man who doesn't love music.
Never marry a man whose plants are all dead.
Never marry a man your mother doesn't like.
Never marry a man your children don't like.
Never marry a man who hates his job.
And so on . . .

Reading this laundry list, I wasn't sure whether to laugh or cry.

Clearly, this was the voice of experience. And it made me think
what, if anything, I could tell my own daughter to keep her from
making a big mistake some day.

Of course, Hannah is only 11 and still looks at boys the way she
looks at toadstools after a rainstorm. (Interesting, but not terribly
attractive.)

Still, I already identify with comedian Bill Engvall. On a recent
episode of his sitcom, he told his teenage daughter—to her utter
mortification—that her date honking the horn out front needed to
come inside and meet her parents first.

He does, but before the boy leaves Engvall pulls him aside and
says, "That's my only daughter right there, and she is precious to
me. So if you've got any ideas about *making out* or *hooking up* or
whatever you call it these days, I just want you to know . . . I have
no problem going back to prison."

I know a few fathers who can identify with that sentiment.

But the problem with the "never marry a man . . . " list is that
it approaches the notion of an ideal man from a purely negative
context.

Rather than telling my daughter what to beware of, I'd simply
ask that she marry a gentleman. But then what exactly is a "gentleman" in this day and age?

British-born American writer Oliver Herford once remarked that a gentleman is someone "who never hurts anyone's feelings unintentionally." (This is always said with a wink so that the listener understands that it's okay to insult someone, as long as the slight is intended and the recipient deserving.)

Another wag defined a gentleman as, "someone who knows how to play the accordian, but chooses not to."

We could use a bit more specificity here. And in that department, it's hard to top John Walter Wayland's definition written back in 1899:

> The True Gentleman is the man whose conduct proceeds from good will and an acute sense of propriety, and whose self-control is equal to all emergencies; who does not make the poor man conscious of his poverty, the obscure man of his obscurity, or any man of his inferiority or deformity; who is himself humbled if necessity compels him to humble another; who does not flatter wealth, cringe before power, or boast of his own possessions or achievements; who speaks with frankness but always with sincerity and sympathy; whose deed follows his word; who thinks of the rights and feelings of others, rather than his own; and who appears well in any company, a man with whom honor is sacred and virtue safe.

Pretty much says it all, doesn't it?

Perhaps the important thing for all single men and women is to look inward and cultivate these qualities of character. Doing so might make them worthy to receive the affections of their ideal mate, should they have the good fortune of encountering him or her.

Dr. Randy Pausch, who succumbed to pancreatic cancer last year at 47, also struggled with these questions.

He left behind this time capsule of advice for his 2-year old daughter Chloe: "When men are romantically interested in you, it's really simple. Just ignore everything they say and only pay attention to what they do."

Good advice. And not a bad way of sizing up people generally. ∎

■ BEYOND SELF-ACTUALIZATION

Throughout the twentieth century, most psychological research focused on the dark and destructive side of human nature, the abnormal, the psychotic.

Abraham Maslow changed that.

Rather than focusing on phobias, neuroses, obsessions, and other mental disorders, the pioneering psychologist studied individuals who lived abundant lives, making the best use of their qualities and capacities and exhibiting the highest levels of mental health.

He called these men and women self-actualizers.

Maslow believed that human beings have a hierarchy of needs. Higher needs are only met when lower ones have been fulfilled.

At the bottom, for example, we have physiological needs like oxygen, food, water, and sleep. Next we have safety and security needs. These include things like a safe neighborhood, a secure and comfortable home, and a regular source of income.

Beyond these, we all require love and belonging. We seek friends, a romantic partner, an affectionate family, social groups, and a sense of community.

Once these needs are met, we look to fulfill our esteem. People everywhere crave freedom, attention, recognition, appreciation, and status.

At this point, however, many individuals stop. Things are pretty comfortable. Life is good. Yet real satisfaction is often lacking for a very specific reason.

"A musician must make music, an artist must paint, a poet must write, if he is to be ultimately happy," said Maslow. "What a man can be, he must be. This need we call self-actualization."

What is it exactly?

Using a qualitative method called "biographical analysis," Maslow defined it by studying an elite group of highly functioning people. He interviewed them and the people around them, and studied their words, acts, and letters.

His group included such luminaries as Albert Einstein, Eleanor Roosevelt, Walt Whitman, William James, Albert Schweitzer, Benedict de Spinoza, and Thomas Jefferson. From his research, Maslow distilled 16 characteristics that epitomize the self-actualizing individual:

1. Openness to experience. Self-actualizers are eager to undergo new experiences and rethink old ideas.
2. An efficient perception of reality. Self-actualizers see things as they really are, not as they imagine or wish them to be.
3. Acceptance of self, nature, and others. Self-actualizers rarely feel anxious, guilty, or ashamed. They are confident in themselves and their ability to solve problems.
4. Spontaneity and naturalness. Self-actualizers are genuine in their relationships. They do not wear masks or play roles.
5. Focus on outside problems. Self-actualizers are not self-obsessed. Their focus is on a general "mission" to which they devote their lives.
6. Detachment and privacy. Self-actualizers crave solitude and time for quiet reflection.
7. Continued freshness or appreciation. The self-actualizing man or woman experiences joy in simple, everyday things: sunsets, starry nights, children laughing, autumn leaves.

8. Peak experiences. Self-actualizers experience strong, positive emotions akin to ecstasy. This may include a deep sense of peacefulness or tranquility.
9. Empathy. Self-actualizers are more willing to listen to and learn from people of any class, race, religion, or ideology.
10. Interpersonal relations. Self-actualizing people tend to have relatively fewer friends, but those relationships are likely to be deep and meaningful.
11. Democratic character. The self-actualizer recognizes we all have strengths and weaknesses, but that we share a common humanity and equality.
12. Discrimination between ends and means. Self-actualizers work to achieve desirable ends, but avoid wrong or hurtful means to achieve them.
13. Philosophical sense of humor. Self-actualizers enjoy humor but not at the expense of others. (As Goethe said, "Men show their character in nothing more clearly than what they think laughable.")
14. Creativity. Self-actualizers enjoy using their creative abilities, whether it's writing, drawing, music, or woodworking. (Maslow once remarked that a first-rate soup is better than a second-rate painting.)
15. Resistance to enculturation. Self-actualizers are not dependent on the opinions of others or the conventions imposed by society. They have a keen sense of who and what they are.
16. Awareness of imperfections. Self-actualizers are not saints. They have weaknesses and shortcomings like everyone else. But they are aware of them.

Self-actualization is not simply a goal. It is a philosophy of life, a continual striving, a process of development.

"One's only rival is one's potentialities," said Maslow. "One's only failure is failing to live up to one's own possibilities. In this sense, every man can be a king."

You achieve this by shunning the safe, the comfortable, the routine—and instead seeking opportunities for growth.

"One can choose to go back toward safety or forward toward growth," wrote Maslow. "Growth must be chosen again and again; fear must be overcome again and again."

Self-actualization means seeing life as a series of choices—and choosing the growth choice each time.

According to Maslow, this uniquely human need is at the core of our nature. It creates meaning in our lives.

Throughout his lifetime, Maslow received numerous honors for his original thinking and his breakthroughs in human psychology. Toward the end of his career, however, he had an epiphany—and reversed himself. Self-actualization is essential. Yet there is another plateau: self-transcendence.

Self-transcendence, Maslow argued, is a meta-need, a higher state of consciousness where we transcend our ego and embrace a fundamental connection with the rest of the world. This transcendence is generally accompanied by intense happiness and well-being, the feeling that one is aware of "ultimate truth" and the unity of all things.

Maslow called self-transcendence the next step in human evolution.

Despite his reputation as a brilliant researcher—Maslow received the second-highest IQ score ever recorded—many of his colleagues were outraged. Critics argued that it was logically impossible for the self to transcend itself. Some referred to self-transcendence as "numinous nonsense," claiming Maslow had abandoned the practical for the mystical.

But perhaps he only fused the two.

In the second century B.C.E., the great Indian sage Pantanjali wrote, "When you are inspired by some great purpose, some extraordinary project, all your thoughts break their bonds; your mind transcends limitations, your consciousness expands in every direction, and you find yourself in a new, great and wonderful world. Dormant forces, faculties and talents become alive, and you discover yourself to be a greater person by far than you ever dreamed yourself to be."

Maslow believed self-transcendence takes us beyond rational self-interest, beyond individual self-actualization—and allows us to do something even more meaningful: help others reach their potential.

Until his death in 1970, Maslow encouraged individuals to develop their innate talents and abilities to their fullest extent. (The field of transpersonal psychology sprang up from his studies.) But he also believed he had discovered a higher wisdom, something greater than self-actualization.

"The true value of a human being," said Albert Einstein, "is determined primarily by the measure and the sense in which he has attained liberation from the self."

Sounds transcendent to me.   ■

THE LAST LESSON
OF CULTURE

Not long after graduating from college, I took a job selling ocean-front condominiums in Florida.

I had never worked in sales before, but this seemed like a good place to start. The units were beautiful. The view out back was unbeatable. And there was no prospecting involved. Instead, the developer brought prospects onsite for us to tour.

At the end of my first month, our manager posted a ranking of all the associates by sales volume. To my utter mortification, I was dead last.

If I were going to keep my job, I knew I had to do something and quick. But what? I looked at the top of the rankings and saw that the number one associate was an older gentleman named Don Traster.

With all the stealth of a rogue elephant, I began shadowing Don whenever he gave a tour, eavesdropping at every opportunity. It didn't take long for me to realize why he was so damn good.

It wasn't that he had some incredible sales pitch. Nor was he the stereotypical smooth-talking salesman. Quite the opposite . . .

His real strength was that he had an almost preternatural calmness about him. Sure, he was an experienced salesman. But when Don Traster spoke, he used the kind of soft, quiet tone that a trusted doctor uses to discuss your test results with you. His whole demeanor put you at ease. His soft voice and direct, emotionless delivery not only eliminated any sales pressure whatsoever, it also conveyed enormous credibility.

The man's calmness put everyone under a spell. There was something magnetic about it. And his hapless sales prospects went down like Japanese zeros over Guadalcanal. If you could afford an oceanfront condo and Don Traster was showing you the property, trust me, you were buying one.

I'm sure Don's technique was unconscious. But it was far from unique. In 1902, James Allen published his classic book, *As a Man Thinketh*. In it he revealed that "The more tranquil a man becomes, the greater is his success, his influence, his power for good. Even the ordinary trader will find his business prosperity increase as he develops a greater self-control and equanimity, for people will always prefer to deal with a man whose demeanor is strongly equable."

That's not always easy in our hectic, deadline-oriented world. How do you remain calm in a nonstop whirlwind of quotas, meetings, appointments, emails, and cell phones. According to Allen, it starts by changing your thoughts:

> Nothing can come from corn but corn, nothing from nettles but nettles. Men understand this law in the natural world, and work with it; but few understand it in the mental and moral world. . . . A man is literally what he thinks, his character being the complete sum of all his thoughts.

Some folks will argue that their stressful thoughts are merely the result of personal circumstances. That's not necessarily true, however. We all have a tendency to spin a narrative around whatever is happening to us.

"The primary cause of unhappiness is never the situation but your thoughts about it," writes Eckhart Tolle in *A New Earth*. "Instead of making up stories, stay with the facts. For example, 'I am ruined' is a story. It limits you and prevents you from taking effective action. 'I have fifty cents left in my bank account' is a fact. Facing facts is always empowering. Be aware that what you think, to a large extent, creates the emotions you feel."

Those emotions, in turn, create feelings of either anxiety or serenity. Don Traster's calmness, for example, wasn't feigned. His ordinary demeanor was a combination of alertness and complete unflappability. Those qualities have a powerful allure both inside the business world and beyond.

"That exquisite poise of character which we call serenity is the last lesson of culture," writes Allen. "It is the flowering of life, the fruitage of the soul. It is precious as wisdom, more to be desired than gold. . . . How insignificant mere money-making looks in comparison with a serene life."

No one wants to feel harried or stressed out, of course. But the paradox is that tranquility is not only desirable for its own sake, but subtly attracts the very opportunities the stressed-out majority is out chasing.

So slow down. And remember the words of psychologist William James, "The great discovery of my generation is that human beings can alter their lives by altering their attitudes of mind."   ■

WEALTH THAT CAN'T BE TALLIED

Earlier this year I visited Rancho Santana, a charming resort community on the Pacific coast of Nicaragua, near the town of San Juan del Sur.

Set on more than two miles of coastline with rolling hills and dramatic cliffs, the reserve attracts expats, investors, surfers, and nature lovers from all over the world. They like the idea of owning a piece of—or at least visiting—one of the most spectacular stretches of coastal land in the world.

Gaze out from atop one of the many bluffs on this 2700-acre reserve and you'll see what the coast of California looked like a hundred years ago, pristine and undeveloped.

On the drive here from the historic colonial city of Granada, however, you'll see something else.

Nicaragua is the poorest country in Central America. Approximately half the population lives on the equivalent of less than one dollar a day.

The scene is familiar to anyone who has traveled the back roads of Latin America: There are miles of ramshackle homes with dirt floors, no electricity, and no running water. Women use rocks to pound the laundry clean in streams that run alongside their homes. Half-dressed children without shoes run through scattered livestock. Men fish with lines attached to pieces of wood, since they don't have rods or reels.

To Western eyes unaccustomed to traveling here, it looks desperately bleak. Yet there is something else here you can't escape noticing. Most of the people seem genuinely happy. Kids play with no less abandon than kids anywhere else. Men and women greet you with a nod, a toothy grin, and a pleasant "buenos dias." Their eyes smile. They laugh a lot.

Larry, an attorney from La Jolla who married a local, told me about the first time he invited his wife's family over for dinner. There was a terrific rainstorm and since the river was high and her family had no transportation, he was afraid they wouldn't make it. He needn't have worried, he said. He could hear them approaching two blocks away, laughing and singing, covered with mud.

Most Americans have difficulty imaging the daily struggle of these people. Yet they aren't miserable. Far from it.

"It's true, the poor are genuinely happy here," says my friend Horacio Marquez, an Argentine who has lived and traveled throughout Latin America. "To us, it looks like they have nothing. But they draw tremendous strength from their families, their Catholic faith and their community."

It's a sad irony that so many in The Land of Material Comfort suffer from discontent, anxiety, and neuroses while the folks here earning a subsistence living off the land and the sea seem relaxed and cheerful.

Some will argue that you can't miss what you never had, what you wouldn't even dare to dream. But something more is going on here.

The stoic philosopher Epictetus said, "Learn to wish that everything should come to pass exactly as it does."

His student Marcus Aurelius agreed. "The first rule is to keep an untroubled spirit. The second is to look things in the face and know them for what they are."

This is not just a practical mindset. For Nicaraguans, it is a way of life. When you can't make the world conform to your desires, your best option is to moderate those desires—and seek contentment within. Happiness, it turns out, is an inside-out job.

Satisfaction from fulfilling material wants, on the other hand, is always short-lived. This idea was widespread in the ancient world: Buddha in India and the Stoic philosophers in ancient Greece and Rome counseled people to break their emotional attachment to status and material wealth and cultivate an attitude of acceptance instead.

To some, this sounds defeatist. But what's the point in railing against circumstances that can't be altered? More often than not, changing your mind is a more effective strategy than changing the world.

I don't mean to romanticize the living conditions of these Nicaraguans, incidentally. This is tough living. Literacy rates are low. The infant mortality rate is high. Many Nicaraguans lack access to basic education and essential health care.

Still, you can't help but admire the dignity and spirit here.

As the British essayist Erich Heller observed, "Be careful how you interpret the world; it *is* like that." ■

■ STUMBLING ON HAPPINESS

The recent decline in home values and the stock market, not to mention corporate and municipal bond markets, has left many investors with less than they once had.

To meet their long-term investment goals, many will have to spend less and save more than they originally planned.

This is not easy. As the economist Adam Smith wrote in *The Wealth of Nations* in 1776:

> The desire for food is limited in every man by the narrow capacity of the human stomach; but the desire of the conveniences and ornaments of building, dress, equipage, and household furniture, seems to have no limit or certain boundary.

In this economic downturn, many of us will be unable to afford all the things we want. That will pinch. But should it make us unhappy?

That depends. But for most of us, the answer is a resounding no.

As Harvard psychologist Daniel Gilbert writes in *Stumbling On Happiness*:

> Economists and psychologists have spent decades studying the relation between wealth and happiness, and they have generally concluded that wealth increases human happiness when it lifts people out of abject poverty and into the middle class but that it does little to increase happiness thereafter. Americans who earn $50,000 per year are much happier than those who earn $10,000

per year, but Americans who earn $5 million per year are not much happier than those who earn $100,000 per year. People who live in poor nations are much less happy than people who live in moderately wealthy nations, but people who live in moderately wealthy nations are not much less happy than people who live in extremely wealthy nations. Economists explain that wealth has "declining marginal utility," which is a fancy way of saying that it hurts to be hungry, cold, sick, tired, and scared, but once you've bought your way out of these burdens, the rest of your money is an increasingly useless pile of paper.

If this is true, why are so many people out there busting their humps for more?

For some, it is the sheer challenge of the work or the pursuit of financial independence, both worthy goals. But for others, the answer lies in their increasingly materialistic ways.

We all must consume to survive, of course. But when consumerism becomes an end in itself, when it overruns more important ideals, provides the measure of our success, or corrodes our capacity to know truth, see beauty, or feel love, our lives are diminished.

Some will argue that for economies to flourish, we need rampant consumerism. It is consumers' insatiable hunger for *more stuff* that fuels the economic engine.

In many ways, this is true. In fact, the notion itself is hardly new. In 1759, Adam Smith wrote in *The Theory of Moral Sentiments*:

> The pleasures of wealth and greatness . . . strike the imagination as something grand and beautiful and noble, of which the attainment is well worth all the toil and anxiety which we are so apt to bestow upon it . . . It is this deception which rouses and keeps in continual motion the industry of mankind.

Notice that Smith, the father of free markets, refers to the endless pursuit of *more* as "this deception." He recognized that the needs of a vibrant economy and the requirements for personal contentment are not the same.

Studies show that the riches and material goods we desire—should we have the good fortune to acquire them—won't make us happy for long. Yet we often imagine they will, even when experience teaches us otherwise.

Walk into your local auto dealership, for example, and check out the cars in the show room. They look sharp. They smell good. The tires have been blackened. The exteriors have been waxed, polished, and Windexed until they gleam. In short, we are seduced by their newness.

And even though we know a new automobile is the world's fastest depreciating asset—and within weeks we will be mindlessly traveling from point A to B without a second thought about our vehicle's make or model—we plunk for one.

As my grandmother used to say, "most people can't tell the difference between what they *want* and what they *need*."

(This remark, incidentally, was generally directed toward me—and my latest six-dollar object of fascination—at F. W. Woolworth's.)

Look around today and you'll have no problem finding folks with plenty of neat things: big cars, fancy boats, the latest electronic gadgets, and all sorts of expensive "bling." They seem to have it all.

What you may not realize is how many of them are two payments from the edge . . .

Yet some middle-class Americans remain obsessed with what they don't have. To some, it just doesn't seem right—doesn't seem fair—that others have so much more than they do.

But as political satirist P. J. O'Rourke observed:

> I have a 10 year old at home, and she is always saying, "That's not fair." When she says that, I say, "Honey, you're cute; that's not fair. Your family is pretty well off; that's not fair. You were born in America; that's not fair. Honey, you had better pray to God that things don't start getting fair for you." ∎

The True Meaning
of Success

Over the past several months, the headlines have been full of economic misery.

Foreclosure filings have hit a record. Repo lots overflow with reclaimed cars. And, according to the *Washington Post,* personal bankruptcies are up more than 40 percent.

Some of those hardest hit are enduring a perfect storm in the economy: higher prices, a weak job market, rising mortgage payments, falling home values, and tougher lending standards.

Others, however, are suffering for a different reason. They chased a blinkered image of success: the idea that status and self-worth are derived from flashy cars, expensive jewelry, or a five-bedroom McMansion in a gated community.

If you can afford these things, fine. Enjoy them. But if they are a struggle, could they really be worth long hours, strained relationships, or your kids continually asking, "Where's Dad?"

Life is short and time expended earning a living is, in effect, trading life for cash. We all have an overhead, of course. But what else are you trading your life for?

I once heard a customer in a jewelry shop asking the store manager just how accurate the Rolex was he was considering.

"Sir," he answered, "I'm more than happy to tell you about the amazing Swiss craftsmanship that goes into each of these timepieces.

But, in truth, nothing under this counter keeps time as well as the cell phone in your pocket."

This man knew his business. He wasn't selling watches. He was selling luxury, a certain image of success.

There's nothing wrong with that. The world is full of desirable things. But some of us have forgotten that the important things in life aren't things at all. And genuine success cannot be measured in dollars and cents.

As Bob Dylan once said, "What's money? A man is a success if he gets up in the morning and goes to bed at night and in between does what he wants to do."

"What is success?" asked Ralph Waldo Emerson, "To laugh often and much. To win the respect of intelligent people and the affection of children. To earn the appreciation of honest critics and endure the betrayal of false friends. To appreciate beauty. To find the best in others. To leave the world a bit better, whether by a healthy child, a garden patch or a redeemed social condition. To know even one life breathed easier because you have lived; this is to have succeeded."

Yet many in society equate success with money and possessions. This is not just a modern phenomenon. There has always been fierce competition for resources. Citizens of ancient Greece and Rome hungered for wealth and power, too.

What has changed dramatically is today's level of material prosperity, fueled in part by access to easy credit. Unfortunately, the quest for *more* can quickly overtake your priorities.

Nearly 150 years ago, philosopher Arthur Schopenhauer wrote in *The Wisdom of Life*:

> It is manifestly a wiser course to aim at the maintenance of our health and the cultivation of our faculties, than at the amassing of wealth . . . Beyond the satisfaction of some real and natural necessities, all that the possession of wealth can achieve has a very small influence upon our happiness, in the proper sense of the word; indeed, wealth rather disturbs it, because the preservation of property entails a great many unavoidable anxieties.

And still men are a thousand times more intent on becoming rich than on acquiring culture, though it is quite certain that what a man *is* contributes much more to his happiness than what he *has*. So you may see many a man, as industrious as an ant, ceaselessly occupied from morning to night in the endeavor to increase his heap of gold . . .

And if he is lucky, his struggles result in his having a really great pile of gold, which he leaves to his heir, either to make it still larger, or to squander it in extravagance. A life like this, though pursued with a sense of earnestness and an air of importance, is just as silly as many another which has a fool's cap for its symbol. *What a man has in himself* is, then, the chief element in his happiness.

The desire to have, to acquire, and to possess, is in principle insatiable. Yet rarely does it generate the fulfillment we imagine. By contrast, doing, creating, contributing, or giving *does* generate the sense of satisfaction we crave.

In setting our priorities, therefore, shouldn't doing precede having? After all, how can you *do* what you really *want* if you're too busy *working* for what you *have*.

So check your priorities. Make sure your actions are in sync with them. As essayist Christopher Morley observed a century ago, "There is only one success—to be able to spend your life in your own way." ■

PART TWO

WHAT MATTERS MOST

The tough economy is forcing a lot of families to make hard choices right now. That doesn't mean they have to be poor ones, however.

Eight years ago, for instance, I left the money management business to write about the financial markets for Agora Publishing.

I needed to re-pot myself. And when my friend and former colleague Steve Sjuggerud decided to step down as Investment Director of The Oxford Club to start a hedge fund, I had the opportunity.

There were drawbacks, however. The starting salary was only a small fraction of what I was currently making. The job security wasn't as great either.

I left anyway. And I'm glad I did.

I've met hundreds of new people. I spend my days doing what I love most. Doors opened up that I could never have imagined when I first took the job. I've traveled the globe, from Europe and South America to Africa and the Orient. After years of being chained to my telephone and my "quote machine," I was free at last.

Last summer I made another leap. After 28 years living in central Florida, my wife, Karen, and I decided to move our family to Charlottesville, VA—just to try it out.

"You've only lived here seven months?" a woman I'd just met asked. "I assume your job brought you here."

"No," I said.

"You have family here in Charlottesville?"

"No."

"You had friends here?"

"No."

"Really?" she persisted. "Who did you know here in town?"

"No one, actually."

From her expression, you'd have thought she'd just identified someone in the federal witness protection program.

There were plenty of good reasons we moved here, of course. Unlike Florida, there are four gorgeous seasons. (Well, three. I'm still not crazy about that one before spring.) Charlottesville is a charming town with tons of culture—thanks to the University of Virginia—and no big-city problems.

The majestic Blue Ridge sits just west of town, providing spectacular sunsets. In 20 minutes, I can be hiking the Appalachian Trail. And I have family in Staunton less than an hour away.

It hasn't been a completely smooth transition, of course. There's no major airport here. We're renting a furnished house (and learning just how little of "all that stuff" back in Florida we really need).

The toughest part was leaving friends we've known for most of our lives. But we still go back to visit. And we're already making new ones. It looks like we're here to stay.

People we meet often tell us they dream of doing something like this. Only money holds them back, they say.

But does it really? If you're willing to make some tough choices, you might be able to downsize to a far more enjoyable and less stressful lifestyle.

That may mean moving from the big city to a more affordable town, going from a three- or four-bedroom house to something smaller, trading two cars for one—or for public transportation.

Some wouldn't consider such a move because "it's too risky" or they're concerned what other people might think. But giving up the life you could be leading in order to live up to someone else's expectations is a terrible tradeoff.

Only you can determine what's most important—and arrange your circumstances to make it happen. The payoff is you get to live an authentic life.

Thinking about *what matters most* is a good place to start.

■ What's on Your Bucket List?

In the 2007 film *The Bucket List*, Jack Nicholson and Morgan Freeman play two men sharing a hospital room who have little in common, except for their terminal illnesses.

With only months to live, they hit the road with a wish list of things to do before they "kick the bucket."

In Hollywood, of course, that means racecar driving, skydiving, climbing the pyramids, and motorcycling the Great Wall of China.

Some items on their lists, however, are less easily achieved: rekindling a lackluster marriage, reconciling with an estranged daughter, and so on.

The film was only a mixed success given the star power of the two leading actors. But it did spark a lot of conversation . . .

Smithsonian magazine featured "28 Places to See Before You Die." John Izzo wrote *The Five Secrets You Must Discover Before You Die*. Other books offer the 1,000 foods you must taste, the 1,000 recordings you must hear, and the 1,000 paintings you must see before you die.

(Sounds like a lot of pressure.)

The idea of creating and managing a bucket list quickly caught on. According to the *New York Times*, over the past three years more than 1.2 million people have posted their personal lists on the website 43Things.com.

Some folks have exotic aspirations: wing-walking, running with the bulls in Pamplona, experiencing weightlessness, visiting Easter Island, or riding the Trans-Siberian Express across Asia.

Others are more down-home: start a garden, enter a marathon, see the Aurora Borealis, write an autobiography, ride in a hot air balloon, give an anonymous $1,000 to charity.

Still others are a little more "out there": Search for extraterrestrials. Inhale helium and sing "Yellow Submarine." Join the 300 Club at the South Pole. (That one entails taking a sauna to 200 degrees and then running naked to the pole in minus 100 degree weather.)

Many people enjoy swapping bucket list recommendations . . .

For instance, you haven't really lived, in my opinion, if you haven't peered over the rim of the Grand Canyon, read *The Code of the Woosters*, enjoyed a candlelight dinner to the sound of *John Coltrane & Johnny Hartman*, or visited the north point of Anna Maria Island to watch the sun set.

Of course, the reason for a bucket list is to get away from what someone else wants and finally do what you want.

What's the process? According to my research—which includes nearly twenty minutes of digging around online—here's how to create and manage your bucket list:

1. Make your goals realistic and achievable.
2. Put your list in writing and review it regularly.
3. Don't be reluctant to change or modify it.
4. Planning is not optional. After making your list, decide exactly how and when you intend to get there.
5. Cross off each item as you achieve it.
6. If you live long enough, repeat.

Some may feel a list like this is self-indulgent. After all, folks are busy. They have commitments and responsibilities. Where is the time for a cooking class, blue marlin fishing, or a reef dive?

Ironically, these are the people who would benefit the most from this exercise.

Are we really too guilt-ridden or tied to the grindstone to live life on our own terms? Will we delude ourselves that we will get around to doing the things we really want "eventually"?

As Ralph Waldo Emerson said, "We are always getting ready to live, but never living."

We all have obligations, true. But life can't just be about pleasing your parents, your boss, your spouse, and your children. It has to be about more than meeting your quota, making the mortgage, picking up the kids, and socking something away for a rainy day.

For too many of us, there is a gap between how we spend our time and what is really important.

If you have a friend or partner who shares your dreams, that's great. But sometimes it takes courage to do what you want. Other people have a lot of plans for you. They want you to go on "their trip."

Mythologist Joseph Campbell described this as a slave morality, a path to disintegration of both body and spirit. "We must be willing to get rid of the life we've planned," he said, "so as to have the life that is waiting for us."

Some people miss this entirely. They're too busy making a living to make a life. Others understand it perfectly. Oscar Wilde said, "I've put my genius into my life; I've only put my talent into my work."

A bucket list requires you to confront your mortality and recognize that you have only so much time to do whatever it is you really want. It makes you stop and enumerate those things. It encourages you to plan for them. And it motivates you.

As management consultant Brian Tracy writes, "When you have clear, exciting goals and ideals, you will feel happier about yourself and your world. You will be more positive and optimistic. You will be more cheerful and enthusiastic. You will feel internally motivated to get up and get going every morning because every step you are taking will be moving you in the direction of something that is important to you."

After all, it's not how fast you're moving, it's where you're headed. A meaningful life is not about speed and efficiency. It is more a matter of what you do and why you do it.

Some individuals aren't comfortable branching out, experimenting with their lives. But by avoiding risk, they risk something even greater: an unlived life.

Survey the residents at your local nursing home, for example, and they will tell you their greatest regrets are not the things they did or the mistakes they made, but rather the things they didn't do, the risks they didn't take.

As the German poet Christian Fürchtegott Gellert advised, "Live as you will have wished to have lived when you are dying."

A bucket list is a step in that direction. It may sound frivolous to some. But is it such a bad idea to jot down what you really want to do before you ditch this mortal coil?

We take so many freedoms for granted. Freedom from regret, however, is up to you.   ■

How to Calculate Your Real Wealth

"It is one of the blessings of old friends," said Ralph Waldo Emerson, "that you can afford to be stupid with them."

This is true. I know because I recently survived one of the stupidest weekends of my life.

Twenty-five of my oldest and dearest friends converged on the Villas of Grand Cypress in Orlando for a weekend of eating, drinking, golfing, and, yes, much stupidity.

Old stories were told. Old lies were repeated. Old insults were traded. (Along with a few new ones.) It was heaven.

This particular group was not my work buddies, my college buddies, my neighborhood buddies, or my tennis buddies. No, these are the derelicts who have stuck with me my whole life. Some of them were in my kindergarten class.

My friend Rick Pfeifer brought his daughter Courtney, a senior at Florida State, to dinner Friday night. I've known Courtney for more than twenty years, too. I used to pick her up and hold her when she was a baby. (I asked Rick if I could pick her up and hold her now. (He said no.)

These are not just long-time companions. These are the guys who will show up at my funeral even if it's raining. (Assuming I don't outlive these alcoholics.)

It has been said many times, but you really can't put a price on friendship. Our true friends are the ones who have known us the longest, understand us the best, yet choose to hang out with us anyway.

Friends like these are irreplaceable. They are the wine of life. The classical world understood this well: "There is nothing on this earth more to be prized than true friendship," said Saint Thomas Aquinas. "Without friends even the most agreeable pursuits become tedious."

The Greek philosopher Antisthenes said, "There are only two people who can tell you the truth about yourself—an enemy who has lost his temper and a friend who loves you dearly."

"It is a good thing to be rich, it is a good thing to be strong," observed the tragedian Euripides, "but it is a better thing to be beloved of many friends."

Yet we don't always appreciate these riches. We can take our friends for granted. We may get too busy or self-involved to check on them, to see how they're doing. Without meaning to, we lose touch.

A few months ago, out of the blue, I received a phone call from my old college roommate, Brian Darby. He invited me to join him—and some other old fraternity buddies—for a weekend at his golf club near Tampa.

I had lost touch with Brian more than twenty-five years ago. He has sons who are the same age he was when I saw him last.

Yet from the first slap on the back, it was clear that no time had really passed. Nothing had changed. It didn't take ten seconds to reconnect—or for us to begin retelling those old stories. In short, much stupidity ensued.

It was bliss.

During the weekend revelry in Orlando, however, our group received the news that political journalist Tim Russert had suddenly collapsed from a heart attack at work and died. He was 58. While none of us knew Russert personally, we were momentarily dumbstruck.

We resolved then and there to stop waiting for a reason and start making plans to get together each year. After all, most of us are already on the back nine. Why wait?

We've chosen this year's organizer. And each year we intend to meet at a different locale for more camaraderie. More fellowship. More stupidity.

How about you? Do you have old friends out there who would be delighted to see you or thrilled—as I was recently—to get an unexpected phone call?

If so, reach out and call them. Meet them for lunch. Be the organizer who pulls your old group together. (Trust me, you'll win extra accolades for that.) Do it—and you are guaranteed a rewarding experience.

After all, these are not our relatives, our neighbors, or our business colleagues. These are the folks above all others that we choose to spend our time with. That doesn't just make them special.

It makes them priceless. ■

THE MOST VALUABLE THING YOU OWN

Many years ago I worked for one of the most charismatic individuals I've ever known.

He was successful in business, gracious, funny, generous, and smart. He was thoughtful too, always inquiring about my family or how things were going.

He was wealthy, well educated, and well traveled. Whenever you bumped into him, it seemed, he was returning from some exotic trip where he had rubbed elbows with Oprah Winfrey or Tom Cruise.

He impressed men. He charmed women. Everyone wanted to be like him. There was only one drawback.

You couldn't always trust him.

I'm not suggesting he was a thief or a crook. He wasn't. But he had personal credibility issues.

He would tell you he was going to do something and not follow through. His stories were often so exaggerated that they bore little relationship to reality.

And if the measure of the man is in small matters, he often came up short. For instance, he would sometimes invite a group of us to his private club for a round of golf. He would pick up the tab for everyone's greens fees, cart fees, lunch, and drinks. And then cheat like the dickens to win the $5 Nassau we were playing.

It was ridiculous.

Over time these ethical lapses affected his business. He never broke contracts or the law. But he operated in grey areas, sometimes treating long-time employees shabbily or using hardball tactics to get his way with business partners.

Eventually, I had a falling out with him and left the company. Looking back I still shake my head. He was such a great guy in so many ways. Yet no matter what someone has going for him in the plus column, nothing compensates for a lack of personal integrity.

In the world of personal and business relationships, reputation is everything. In some ways, it is the most valuable thing you own.

"Who you are speaks so loudly I can't hear what you're saying," wrote Ralph Waldo Emerson two centuries ago.

Reputations, of course, aren't always entirely accurate. But they are a necessary shortcut. It takes time—sometimes years—to truly know someone's character. Decisions and judgments need to be made much sooner. So we depend on reputations.

Whether you're making a new friend or business contact, seeking a new love-interest or applying for a new job, nothing can help or hurt your prospects more than your reputation.

In a sense, your reputation is your ambassador. Every day it is out there circulating, knocking on doors, joining in conversations, arriving well before you do, and paving the way—for good or ill.

Your reputation affects the way the world perceives and interprets much of what you do. A couple hundred years ago, a man would challenge another to a duel if he felt his integrity had been insulted. Reputation was beyond value. A serious slight could not be allowed to stand.

In reality, of course, your reputation is only what others imagine you are. Your character is what you truly are. In my experience, however, long-standing reputations are generally pretty accurate—and good ones are almost impossible to manufacture. People are too smart for that.

As Emerson said, "The louder he talked of his honor, the faster we counted our spoons."

Our deeds define us, not our words. If we wish to burnish our reputation, we have to work on our character. Not a bad idea, either. This is an area, if we are honest with ourselves, where we all could use a little home improvement.

Building character means taking responsibility, being accountable and treating others with fairness and respect, especially those who can do nothing for us in return.

Even then, reputations are built painstakingly, one step at a time. That's why we should never participate in malicious gossip. You don't want to inflict unwarranted damage on someone else's reputation.

And no one ever raised his own reputation by lowering someone else's. Quite the opposite, in fact. As the German writer Jean Paul Richter observed, "A man never discloses his character so clearly as when he describes another's."

Every day, without being consciously aware of it, each of us is enhancing or diminishing our reputation through our actions. Those actions, in turn, are determined by the quality of our thoughts.

As Charles Reader famously said, "Sow a thought, and you reap an act; sow an act, and your reap a habit; sow a habit, and you reap a character; sow a character, and you reap a destiny."

The Greek philosopher Heraclitus was pithier. He simply said that character is destiny. His words are as true today as when he wrote them 2,500 years ago.

Our destiny is fixed when we hold ourselves to a higher standard, follow the dictates of conscience, and do the right thing—especially when another path would be so much easier.

Or, as investor Warren Buffett once remarked, "It takes 20 years to build a reputation and five minutes to ruin it. If you think about that, you'll do things differently."   ■

THE BIGGEST QUESTION

It's an age-old question. Perhaps *the* age-old question.

What is the meaning of life?

Late one night during my freshmen year at college, a loud group in my dorm set out to resolve the question once and for all. Forceful, confident opinions ensued.

However, as I was clearing the beer cans off the floor the next morning, I couldn't recall that any particular light was shed on the subject.

As Kurt Vonnegut would say, "And so it goes."

We weren't the only deep thinkers who failed on this front. Theologians have wrestled with the question for centuries. Philosophers and their students have tied themselves in knots over it. Mystics have eaten mushrooms and meditated on it. Even Monty Python took a stab at it. Still . . . no luck.

Let's pick up the trail where Hugh Moorhead left off.

Moorhead was a Professor of Philosophy at Northeastern University. Over the course of more than twenty years, he mailed his favorite books to their authors (most of them well-known intellectuals) for an autograph. Each time he wrote a letter expressing his appreciation of the work and asked the author to inscribe the inside cover with a comment "on the meaning or purpose of life."

Many refused to take the bait.

Physicist and science writer Freeman Dyson responded, "You ask: what is the meaning or purpose of life? I can only answer with another question: do you think we are wise enough to read God's mind?"

Author Cormac McCarthy retorted: "A successful life is one that has no need to ask the question."

Poet T. S. Eliot also took a pass, apologizing for not having got to the point where he could sum it all up on a flyleaf.

But a number of authors took their best shot, some drawing inspiration from their religious beliefs. For example, Harvey Cox, author of *The Seduction of the Spirit,* said, "The purpose of life is to glorify God and enjoy Him forever."

Other responses were more secular. Leonard Bernstein wrote: "For me, the purpose of life is to live it as fully as possible and be grateful every day for the privilege of sharing it."

Western writer Louis L'Amour said, "The meaning and purpose of life? To *do,* and to *become.*"

American educator Paul Arthur Schlipp wrote it "is to achieve a high development and integration of reason, of morality, and of spirituality—and to commit one's self to a cause greater than one's self. Tell me what your cause is, and I will tell you who you are."

Quite a few of Moorhead's respondents argued that there is no single "answer" to this thorniest of questions.

Steven M. Cahn, author of *Fate, Logic and Time,* insisted, "The meaning of life is invented, not discovered."

Others concurred, writing variations on this theme. Science writer Isaac Asimov was one, adding, "It is always possible for an individual to invest his own life with meaning that he can find significant. He can so order his life that he may find as much beauty and wisdom in it as he can, and spread as much of that to others as possible."

Similarly, Paul Kurtz, author of *The Transcendental Temptation,* wrote, "The meanings that we untap in life are those that we create, the dreams, plans and projects that we live for. How exciting these can be are a measure of our imagination and creativity."

In all, Moorhead received dozens of thought-provoking answers. Over the years I've heard many more, some of them hilarious.

For sheer bullheadedness, for example, Gertrude Stein is hard to beat: "There ain't no answer. There ain't gonna be any answer. There never has been an answer. That's the answer."

Stein's view aside, I recently discovered an "answ
nated with me because it comes with an implied kick in the pan...

Australian Matthew Kelly, author of *The Rhythm of Life,* says the essential meaning and purpose of life is to become "the best-version-of-yourself."

Kelly reminds us that what we *do* in our lives may bring us financial rewards, status, fame, power, and possessions. But genuine happiness and lasting fulfillment are not the by-product of *doing* and *having.* Who you become is infinitely more important than what you *do* or what you *have.*

Kelly says, "It is the quest to improve ourselves, to be all we are capable of being, to test our limits, and to grow steadily toward the-best-version-of-ourselves that brings meaning to our lives."

There's plenty here to keep us occupied. Think about it. What would it take for you to become your best, physically, intellectually, emotionally, and spiritually?

Decide what that is—in the event that you don't already know—and devote yourself to realizing it. The beauty of this approach is that it takes our minds off judging others and puts us on the road to improving ourselves.

Not coincidentally, this is exactly the message of every great wisdom tradition. As Gandhi said, "Be the change you want to see in the world."

This best-version-of-yourself philosophy can be applied to every area of your life. We all have weaknesses that need attention. But we also have personal strengths. Some of us are built to pursue excellence in athletics. Others have a great aptitude for science or mathematics. Maybe the important thing for you right now is to become the best parent, spouse, son, or daughter you can be. Perhaps you feel your life's mission is to feed the poor or build houses for the homeless. Whatever it is, embrace it.

And don't kid yourself that you're too old . . . or it's too late.

Michelangelo designed the dome of St. Peter's Basilica in Rome when he was 72. Nelson Mandela was 75 when he was elected president of South Africa. Benjamin Franklin was 79 when he invented bifocals. Frank Lloyd Wright completed his work on the Guggenheim Museum when he was 91. And Don Byerly was a 103 when he finally climbed to the summit of Mt. Everest.

(Okay, I made up that last one. But the others are good.)

Whatever your station in life, you can find purpose, meaning, and direction by committing to becoming the best version of yourself. Where your unique talents intersect with the world's needs, there you will find your mission.

As Robert Louis Stevenson said more than a century ago, "To be what we are, and to become what we are capable of becoming, is the only end in life." ∎

DREAMS WITH DEADLINES

We all dream. And our dreams tell the world—and ourselves—who we really are.

Some of us dream of financial independence. Others of traveling the world. Or learning to play the piano. Retiring to the country. Raising money for cancer research. Becoming an expert on wine. Writing that novel. Learning to speak Spanish.

Of course, if you aren't pursuing your dreams, the real question is what's stopping you?

For many of us, it is a lack of specificity . . . and a deadline. Our thinking is too nebulous. What we need are realistic, well-articulated goals. Dreams with deadlines.

For example, "I want a comfortable retirement" is a wish. "I want to have a $1 million net worth on my 65th birthday" is a goal.

"I'd like to do something for charity" may be a heartfelt desire. But "I want to raise $30,000 for the International Rescue Committee by December 31st" is a definite end.

Goals give your life meaning and direction. They focus your time and energy. They shape and set your priorities, giving you a reason to get up in the morning.

Without them, we tend to drift. Millions of Americans, for instance, have fallen into a largely meaningless cycle of eating, sleeping, working, and watching TV. After a while, a sort of existential ennui sets in.

But when you have a goal that inspires you—whether its traveling to all fifty states, reading the world's great books, or meeting the person you want to spend the rest of your life with—you feel motivated. Goals are empowering. You know exactly what you want and the idea of attaining it energizes you.

As the English novelist Charles Kingsley observed, "We act as though comfort and luxury were the chief requirements of life, when all that we need to make us really happy is something to be enthusiastic about."

Transcendentalist Henry David Thoreau agreed. He said, "If one advances confidently in the direction of his dreams, and endeavors to live the life which he has imagined, he will meet with success unexpected in common hours."

Of course, setting goals and achieving them are two different things.

A few years ago, I saved an article by author Michael Masterson titled "How to Accomplish All Your Most Important Goals . . . Without Fail."

Here, essentially, is what he said:

1. Take out a sheet of paper. Title it "Life's Goals" (if you have no shame) or "Stuff to Do Before I Croak" (if you are afraid someone will see it).
2. Now make a list of everything you want to accomplish.
3. Narrow your list down to four main goals. Think in terms of a long-term wealth-building goal, a long-term health goal, a long-term personal-relationship goal, and a long-term personal growth and development goal. These are your top priorities, your bottom-line objectives.
4. Convert these into annual goals and then break them down further into manageable, bite-sized weekly objectives.
5. Once a week, spend one hour establishing your priorities for the next seven days.
6. Finally, spend about 30 minutes each morning organizing your day around them.

His approach is straightforward: Dream it. Plan it. Do it.

"It may sound like a lot," says Masterson, "but you're really spending no more than the equivalent of a few days a year to map out your strategy for achieving your long-term Life Goals.

"When I put my list down on paper, I feel powerful and confident. Here are the things I will accomplish this year. Clean and simple. I imagine how I will feel when they are completed, and that feeling is good . . .

"There is something about this particular system that seems to work. It works so well, in fact, that I encourage everyone who works for me to use it."

Of course, some of us never make an honest attempt to achieve our goals for a single unspoken reason: fear of failure. Yet there is much to be gained in pursuing your dreams, regardless of whether you ultimately achieve them.

"The tragedy of life doesn't lie in not reaching your goal," said African American minister Benjamin Mays. "The tragedy lies in having no goal to reach. It isn't a calamity to die with dreams unfulfilled, but it is a calamity not to dream. It isn't a disgrace not to reach the stars, but it is a disgrace to have no stars to reach for. Not failure, but low aim, is a sin."

So follow Thoreau's advice and go confidently in the direction of your dreams. Live the life that you've imagined.

As Mark Twain observed, "Twenty years from now you will be more disappointed by the things that you didn't do than by the ones you did do. So throw off the bowlines. Sail away from the safe harbor. Catch the trade winds in your sails. Explore. Dream. Discover." ■

THE MOST BEAUTIFUL PLACE ON EARTH?

Is it possible for a place to be spiritual? Not a church, a shrine, or a tabernacle, but just an area of incredible natural beauty?

I set out to answer that question last spring when I drove south on Scenic Highway One from Monterey with my colleague Steven King. We were on our way to Big Sur, the famous 90-mile stretch of rugged and beautiful coastline between Carmel and San Simeon.

Steven had never been there before. "What are we going to do when we get there?" he asked, a bit apprehensive.

"Just look," I said.

"You're kidding, right?"

It was a picture-perfect day: 63 degrees, a gentle breeze blowing in off the coast, not a cloud in sight. Suddenly, to the left us were the imposing San Lucia Mountains, and on the right a majestic view of the Pacific.

"Holy —," Steven said, dumbstruck as we rounded the first bend.

This is arguably the world's most dramatic meeting of land and sea, an area of unsurpassed natural beauty. For decades, it has attracted painters, sculptors, novelists, and other creative types, including one of my favorite American writers, Henry Miller.

The author of *Tropic of Cancer* and *Stand Still Like the Hummingbird* called Big Sur home from 1944 to 1962. And he clearly drew inspiration here.

"Often, when following the trail which meanders over the hills," he wrote, "I pull myself up in an effort to encompass the glory and the grandeur which envelopes the whole horizon. Often, when the clouds pile up in the north and the sea is churned with white caps, I say to myself, 'This is the California that men dreamed of years ago, this is the Pacific that Balboa looked out on from the Peak of Darien, this is face of the earth as the Creator intended it to look.'"

Steven and I soaked up the vistas for a couple hours, then hiked a few mostly empty trails through the redwoods in Pfeiffer Big Sur State Park. Afterwards, we stopped in for a bit of browsing at the local Henry Miller Library. "Check your neuroses and psychoses at the gate," reads a sign out front.

Yet it's tough having a genuine Miller memorial. For starters, he didn't approve of them. Memorials, he said, "defeated the purpose of a man's life. Only in living your life to the full can you honor the memory of someone."

His own days were certainly full of gusto. As a young man, he lived an impecunious life, roaming the streets of Paris. His entire life, in fact, was nonmaterialistic.

"If there is to be any peace," he once wrote, "it will come through being, not having."

Miller was married five times. (Another good reason he was broke.) He was a painter, an essayist, a pianist, a novelist, and was featured in Warren Beatty's film *Reds*. He spent years studying the world's great religious traditions. And found something to admire in each of them:

"Buddha gave us the eight-fold path. Jesus showed us the perfect life. Lao-Tzu rode off on a water buffalo, having condensed his vast and joyous wisdom into a few imperishable words."

Steven and I knocked about the library for a while—squinting at old photographs, letters, and manuscripts—then headed back out to the cliffs to watch the harbor seals and a school of more than a hundred dolphin, the biggest I've ever seen. (We also searched the sky overhead for the elusive California Condor. No luck.)

We topped off the day with a leisurely lunch and a glass of Sauvignon Blanc at Nepenthe—absolutely recommended—before heading back down the coastline.

So, does a lazy day at an idyllic spot really count as a spiritual experience? I doubt Henry Miller would argue the point. When he died in 1980, he had his ashes scattered off the coast here.

"It was here in Big Sur," he wrote, "I first learned to say Amen!" ■

How to Avoid "The Mañana Syndrome"

Two years ago, one of the nation's largest publishers, John Wiley & Sons, asked if I would write a book about my investment philosophy. I agreed and they paid me a sizable advance.

Unfortunately, I didn't make the first deadline. Or the second. As the third one loomed, executive editor Debra Englander was on the phone. And she wasn't happy.

Was I going to write the book or not?

I said I was. But when? I was already buried in other research and writing projects.

I tried knocking out my short-term deadlines first, so I could turn my attention to the book later in the week. But things kept piling up and "later" never seemed to happen.

It wasn't that I didn't have plenty of material for the book. I did. What's more, I really wanted to do it. I just felt too exhausted at the end of each day to tackle such a big project.

As I traveled with a group of investors through Italy two years ago, I finally conceded that trying to write a book on top of all my other commitments was just crazy. Reluctantly, I decided I would return the advance to Wiley and maybe try again some time when things weren't so hectic.

With me on the trip, however, was an aspiring writer from Tennessee, Richard Nelson, who had recently self-published a book of maxims. As we boarded the coach for the airport the next day, he handed me a copy.

On the first page, my eye fell on the following quote: "There is no shortage of time, only a confusion of priorities." I suddenly felt like I had been struck on the head with a ball-peen hammer.

If I really wanted to do that book, I had to stop wishing I had the time and start making it. In short, I went to war. I delegated some responsibilities to my colleagues. And no matter what was on my schedule each day, it had to wait until I had spent at least a couple hours working on the book.

With all the excuses out of the way and a genuine commitment underway, I finished it in just over five months. The book *The Gone Fishin' Portfolio: Get Wise, Get Wealthy . . . and Get On With Your Life* became a *New York Times* bestseller and was chosen by the editors at Amazon as one of the "Top Ten Business and Investment Books of 2008."

I couldn't have done it if I hadn't stopped deluding myself that I would get around to writing it "eventually." At some point, we all have to recognize that we'll never change our lives for the better—or accomplish the things we really want—until we change something we do daily. This applies to virtually every aspect of life.

Want to rise in your business? Start working harder and learning more about your organization today. Need to put together an estate plan for your family? Call your attorney right now. Want to lose 10 pounds? Start eating better and exercising today. Not tomorrow. Not when you get "one thing" out of the way. Today.

As Gary Buffone writes in *The Myth of Tomorrow*, "The very fact that our time is finite makes living precious. When we exclude the recognition of our end, when we lose sight of the real stakes involved, life becomes impoverished. It becomes easier to develop 'mañana syndrome' and constantly postpone authentic living. People who presume that there is always tomorrow waste away in unproductive and meaningless jobs, joyless relationships, pointless worries, and vague plans for some distant future."

Don't be one of them. If you need encouragement, John Maxwell, author of *Today Matters*, offers a helpful prayer:

> Dear Lord, So far today, I am doing all right. I have not gossiped, lost my temper, been greedy, grumpy, nasty, selfish, or self-indulgent. I have not whined, cursed, or eaten any chocolate. However, I am going to get out of bed in a few minutes, and I will need a lot more help after that. Amen.

According to Maxwell, "People create success in their lives by focusing on today. It may sound trite, but today is the only time you have. It's too late for yesterday. And you can't depend on tomorrow. That's why today matters."

Most of us are planners, of course, and forward-looking by nature. But it's what you do today that determines what you are tomorrow. Or, as the great industrialist Henry Ford once said, "You can't build a reputation on what you're going to do."

So give yourself a friendly push and start pursuing what matters most. Commit to it daily. After all, "there is no shortage of time, only a confusion of priorities." ■

Gentlemen, Stop Your Engines!

While in France a couple of years ago, I bumped into my colleague Addison Wiggin, an American publisher and filmmaker who was living in Paris.

During our chat, he told me about a French co-worker who had just returned from her first trip to the United States. When he asked what was her biggest surprise about America, she said, "I can't believe you eat in your *cars*."

We both had a chuckle over this. To Parisians, eating is a sacrament. Even a short lunch has to include fresh bread, good wine, and time enough to enjoy it.

It's a whole different experience than driving down the highway with a Quarter Pounder and fries in your lap—a soft drink big enough to have an undertow sloshing around in the cup holder—while you lick your fingers between bites so you don't get grease on the wheel.

I'm kidding, of course. Americans don't really eat this way on a regular basis. Do we?

Get ready to cringe. A recent study conducted by John Nihoff, a professor of gastronomy at the Culinary Institute of America, found that among 18- to 50-year-old Americans, roughly a fifth of all eating takes place in the car. Almost as bad, studies show that a significant percentage of the rest occurs in front of the TV.

Look, I don't want to be judgmental. If this is how people really want to take their meals, so be it. Of course, I wouldn't call them meals, necessarily. They're more like "eating occasions." Still, if this is how millions of my fellow Americans choose to receive their daily nourishment, all I can say is . . . "*Vive la France!*"

Face it. The French are smarter than us when it comes to eating. Surveys show they rarely snack. They consume most of their food at meals shared with others. They eat smaller portions and don't come back for seconds. They also linger, spending considerably more time eating than we do. Put these habits together and you have a food culture in which the French consume fewer calories than we do, yet enjoy them far more.

As Michael Pollan writes in his book *In Defense of Food,*

> We forget that, historically, people have eaten for a great many reasons other than biological necessity. Food is also about pleasure, about community, about family and spirituality, about our relationship to the natural world, and about expressing our identity. As long as humans have been taking meals together, eating has been as much about culture as it has been about biology. . . .
>
> It is at the dinner table that we socialize and civilize our children, teaching them manners and the art of conversation. At the dinner table parents can determine portion sizes, model eating and drinking behavior, and enforce social norms about greed and gluttony and waste. . . . The shared meal elevates eating from a mechanical process of fueling the body to a ritual of family and community, from mere animal biology to an act of culture.

In the modern world, agriculture, technology, and the free market have succeeded almost too well. Food today is so easy, so cheap, and so plentiful that we forget our ancestors spent most of their waking hours hunting, growing, producing, and preparing meals. It defined their lives. For hundreds of millions in the Third World, it still does.

If we eat mindlessly, we experience a disconnection. We miss a chance to bond with our friends and family. We lose our deep connection to the earth. We forego an opportunity to give thanks. And that's regrettable.

In *The Pleasures of Eating,* Wendell Berry writes,

> Eating with the fullest pleasure—pleasure, that is, that does not depend on ignorance—is perhaps the profoundest enactment of our connection with the world. In this pleasure we experience and celebrate our dependence and our gratitude, for we are living from mystery, from creatures we did not make and powers we cannot comprehend.

This attitude fosters a more deliberate approach to eating. Our meals become a sort of spiritual practice where gratitude, fellowship, and conversation are more important than simply "strapping on the feedbag." We eat less and enjoy it more. Not coincidentally, we look and feel better, too.

So take your cue from the French. Enjoy the company. Savor your meal. And if you really don't have time to eat this way, well . . . don't forget to buckle up.   ∎

ENJOY EVERY SANDWICH

My friend Steve Sjuggerud used to call me occasionally to ask if I'd read any good business or investment books lately.

Since both of us already had shelves groaning with them, it got tougher each year to find new ones that offered any fresh insights. That was before I read Eugene O'Kelly's *Chasing Daylight: How My Forthcoming Death Transformed My Life.*

Four years ago, O'Kelly, the Chairman and CEO of KPMG, one of the largest U.S. accounting firms, was diagnosed with inoperable, late-stage brain cancer. He was told he had three to six months to live.

He was 53.

Suddenly, the life of this rich, powerful, and privileged man, whose days were filled with executive meetings and business appointments, became something very different. *Chasing Daylight* is his memoir, the story of his final journey.

"I'd always aspired to be a Renaissance Man," he writes. "To know about wine and opera, to read books. But after a quarter-century at my firm, I rose to the top position. My life changed. The balance in it faded. Spontaneity died. . . . I was always distracted by work."

Suddenly, he was left with less than 100 days to live. "I had so little time left to learn," he says, "yet—ironically—the first (and maybe the last) thing I needed to learn was how to slow down."

With dignified restraint, O'Kelly describes discovering the world around him—nature, family, friends, living in the moment—as if it were all brand new.

"No more living in the future. (Or the past, for that matter—a problem for many people, although a lesser one for me.) I needed to stop living two months, a week, even a few hours ahead. Even a few minutes ahead. Sixty seconds from now is, in its way, as elusive as sixty years from now, and always will be. It is—was—exhausting to live in a world that never exists. Also kind of silly, since we happen to be blessed with such a fascinating one right here, right now. I felt that if I could learn to stay in the present moment, to be fully conscious of my surroundings, I would buy myself lots of time that had *never* been available to me, not in all the years I was healthy. . . . I would soon discover, though, that staying in the present and being genuinely conscious of my surroundings were just about the hardest things I'd ever attempted."

If you've ever tried to meditate—to still your mind for even a single minute—you know exactly what he's talking about. It's difficult to embrace—and not take for granted—the fleeting moments of our lives.

"Enjoy every sandwich," he writes.

With the clock counting down, O'Kelly makes a list of his closest friends and colleagues and plans a final encounter with each one.

"I stopped at each name and made myself recall, in the closest detail possible, all the moments the two of us had enjoyed together. How we met. What made us become friends in the first place. The qualities in them I particularly appreciated. The lessons I learned by knowing them. The ways in which having met him or her had made me a better person."

His friends were touched—usually overwhelmed—to know how much they had meant to him.

In the course of saying goodbye, he would sometimes invite a friend or acquaintance to take a stroll in the park. This "was sometimes not only the final time we would take such a walk together," he writes, "but also the first time."

Most of us promise ourselves that one day—not too long from now—we'll slow down. We'll spend more time with our family. Enjoy a lazy day out with friends. Or just take a walk alone on the seashore. Some day . . .

If, like me, you're one of the millions who has often deluded himself this way, O'Kelly has just three words of advice: "*Move it up.*"

Eugene O'Kelly died on September 10, 2005.   ■

THE BEST SPIRITUAL
ADVICE

Last April in Washington, D.C., a young man in blue jeans and a T-shirt emerged from the Metro and positioned himself against a wall beside a trash basket.

He removed a violin from a small case, threw in a few dollars and pocket change as seed money, and began to play.

Over the next 45 minutes, more than 1,000 people passed by. Six minutes elapsed before anyone stopped to listen. A crowd never gathered. In fact, only seven people stopped to listen for a minute or more. When he was finished, the young man collected the few extra dollars from his violin case and left.

What's so unusual about this? Nothing, really.

Except that the violinist was no ordinary street performer. It was Joshua Bell, one of the finest classical musicians in the world, playing some of the most elegant music ever written, on one of the most valuable violins ever created, a $3.5 million Stradivarius made in the 1710s.

He was participating in an experiment on "perception and priorities" arranged by the *Washington Post*.

Three days before, Bell had sold out Boston's Symphony Hall, where the cheap seats went for $100 apiece. Two weeks later, he played to a standing-room-only audience at the Music Center at Strathmore, in North Bethesda.

Just how good is Joshua Bell? One prominent music magazine says his playing "does nothing less than tell human beings why we bother to live."

Despite his genius, not 1 percent of more than 1,000 passers-by stopped to listen for even a single minute.

Some folks, of course, will attribute this to the general public's abysmal taste in music. (And a look at the *Billboard* charts might confirm this view.) But something more was going on here. And it has nothing to do with musical tastes or even the hectic pace of modern life.

After all, Helen Keller noticed much the same thing more than 70 years ago—and she was deaf and blind. Writing in the *Atlantic Monthly* in 1933, she said,

> Recently I was visited by a very good friend who had just returned from a long walk in the woods, and I asked her what she had observed. "Nothing in particular," she replied. I might have been incredulous had I not been accustomed to such responses, for long ago I became convinced that the seeing see little.

> How was it possible, I asked myself, to walk for an hour through the woods and see nothing of note? I who cannot see find hundreds of things to interest me through mere touch. I feel the delicate symmetry of a leaf. I pass my hands lovingly about the smooth skin of a birch, or the rough, shaggy, bark of a pine. In spring I touch the branches of trees hopefully in search of a bud. . . . I feel the delightful, velvety texture of a flower. . . . I am delighted to have the cool waters of a brook rush through my open fingers. To me a lush carpet of pine needles or spongy grass is more welcome than the most luxurious Persian rug.

> If I can get so much pleasure from mere touch, how much more beauty must be revealed by sight. Yet, those who have eyes apparently see little. The panorama of color and action which fills the world is taken for granted. It is human, perhaps, to appreciate little that which we have and to long for that which we have not, but it is a great pity that in the world of light the gift of sight is used only as a mere convenience rather than a means of adding fullness to life.

I won't comment further on these two stories. They speak volumes all by themselves.

However, I will add a brief quote from John Horgan, author of *Rational Mysticism:* "The best spiritual advice is the simplest: Pay attention. See! Or rather, cherish. Cherish what you have before it's gone." ∎

Can a Mozart Violin Sonata Change Your Life?

We don't usually think about it, but there is something much *deeper* about hearing than seeing, something that provokes a more powerful emotional response.

In the era of silent movies, for example, a pianist was required to bring out the emotional significance of a love scene.

People who become deaf generally report feeling more isolated than those who become blind.

Studies show that, without sound, we can watch a video of a wounded animal or a person being tortured with relative equanimity. But turn the sound on and—even without the picture—it quickly becomes unbearable.

The human brain is exquisitely sensitive to sound. Yet what do most of us hear in the background each day? Cars honking. Lawnmowers grinding. Dogs barking. Radios blasting. Or the incessant chatter of the idiot box.

I was reminded of this in St. Petersburg Saturday, when I was chatting with my good friend Rustem Hayroudinoff, a Russian classical pianist and Chandos recording artist who, not incidentally, had just blown everyone away the night before with a jaw-dropping performance at the Renaissance Vinoy.

Rustem is a great believer in the spiritual power of great music. He calls it "liquid art." Aside from being a concert performer and recording artist, Rustem teaches at the Royal Academy of Music in London. He told me his toughest job is getting his students, some of whom are headed for international stardom, to understand that music is not just about perfecting the notes. It is about expressing the deepest and most profound human emotions.

"When a member of the audience comes up to me after a performance," Rustem confided, "and says 'I can't believe how fast your fingers were moving' or 'How can you possibly remember all those notes?' I feel like they missed the point, really. But when someone says, 'Rustem, that sonata you played brought tears to my eyes,' I bow my head and say 'thank you' because they understood what I was saying—and they were moved by it."

The wisest among us have always known this. The German poet Berthold Auerbach said "music washes away from the soul the dust of everyday life." Victor Hugo believed music expressed "that which cannot be said and on which it is impossible to be silent." Beethoven called it "the mediator between the spiritual and the sensual life." Nietzsche insisted that without music "life would be a mistake."

Yet the Recording Industry Association tells us that classical music today makes up less than 3 percent of total industry sales. Many of us are so busy working, playing, or rushing to our next appointment that we rarely take even a few minutes to appreciate it.

If this sounds like you, I have a suggestion. Pick up a recording of a Mozart violin sonata. With hundreds of great classical works out there, this may sound needlessly prescriptive, but stick with me a moment.

Mozart was a composer without equal. And his violin sonatas are not only beautiful, they are eminently listenable—even to those who claim to have no taste for serious music.

Tchaikovsky said, "Mozart is the highest, the culminating point that beauty has attained in the sphere of music."

Albert Einstein said, "The music of Mozart is of such purity and beauty that one feels he merely found it—that it has always existed as part of the inner beauty of the universe waiting to be revealed."

Don't get me wrong. I'm not a music snob. When I go to the beach, I want to hear Bob Marley. If I'm having friends over for a barbecue, I'm likely to put on Van Morrison or Miles Davis.

But find a quiet moment to put on a Mozart violin sonata and, instantly, the whole atmosphere changes. The room becomes an oasis of calm sophistication. Put it on in your car and instead of feeling frustrated that you're stuck in traffic, you're grateful to have a few quiet minutes to contemplate something beautiful.

Serious listeners might fume that I'm suggesting you use these immortal works as mood music, a kind of sonic wallpaper. I'm not.

Yes, it may start out that way. But the longer you listen, the more that will be revealed to you. Harmonies and melodies that escaped you at first eventually become obvious. Keep listening and, at some point, you will be struck by the almost mathematical beauty of it all.

I don't mean to rhapsodize here. True, I'm a music lover. But I'm only pointing the way toward something that can have a powerful, positive impact on you each day.

As Anthony Storr writes in *Music and the Mind,* "Music exalts life, enhances life, and gives it meaning . . . It is an irreplaceable, undeserved, transcendental blessing."

So get your hands on a Mozart violin sonata. The human response to organized sound is a mysterious—some would say highly spiritual—thing. No one truly understands it.

As Aldous Huxley famously said, "After silence that which comes nearest to expressing the inexpressible is music." ■

HOW TO TRANSFORM
YOUR LIFE

Bob Williams, a fellow editor at Agora Publishing, has been follow-ing a disciplined meditation practice for more than two years.

He says it helps him stay calm, clear, and focused on the present moment.

It shows. Although he has a mountain of responsibilities, I never see him looking harried, tense, or anxious.

Perhaps he's onto something.

After all, the present moment is all we have. There was never a time when your life was *not* now, nor will there ever be. Your life is and always will be "this moment."

The odd thing about this realization is that it is both bone-crushingly obvious and, at the same time, seldom acknowledged.

Each day we're caught up in our own personal dramas. We struggle to meet the deadline, finish the project, make the appoint-ment, pick up the kids, drop off the car, stop at the bank, visit the folks, plan the dinner. . . . Motoring around, we are swept up in recollections of the past or, more likely, endless planning about the future.

By living in a state of distraction, we deny ourselves the only time we have to be fully present. Right now.

Trust me, you cannot savor your Asian chicken salad with water chestnuts and sliced tangerines if you're worrying about next week's budget meeting. Nor can you enjoy your afternoon by the lake with your grandson if you're talking on your cell phone or fuming about the reset rate on your mortgage.

You can only appreciate the good things in your life when you're fully present. Doing this allows you to minimize the negatives, too.

All of us face situations that are depressing, frustrating, or maddening. Yet, more often than not, our anxieties are the result of our own faulty thinking. It may be tough to admit, but it is our mindset—rather than the situation itself—that creates negative emotions.

As Shakespeare wrote, "There is nothing either good or bad, but thinking makes it so." Truly, it is your thoughts that torment you, not your problems.

Some may disagree. After all, if you have a child with a serious drug addiction or a parent who is dying of cancer, the problem isn't in your mind. It's real.

But there are only two kinds of bad situations in this world: those that can be solved and those that can't. If you have a situation that can be solved, get busy fixing it. If you have one that can't, get busy accepting it.

After all, your thoughts determine your happiness. The good news is that you can control them. That's the power behind Reinhold Niebuhr's well-known Serenity Prayer:

> Grant me the Serenity to accept the things I cannot change;
> Courage to change the things I can; and Wisdom to know the difference.

Incidentally, while Niebuhr wrote this prayer roughly 70 years ago, there is a rhyme dating back to 1695 that expresses a remarkably similar sentiment:

> For every ailment under the sun
> There is a remedy, or there is none;
> If there be one, try to find it;
> If there be none, never mind it.

But when something truly sad or tragic happens, how do you keep from minding it? There is no easy answer to this one. Some wounds only time can heal. But returning to the present moment can help.

As Eckhart Tolle writes in *The Power of Now*, "Narrow your life down to this moment. Your life situation may be full of problems—most life situations are—but find out if you have any problem at this moment. Not tomorrow or in ten minutes, but now. Do you have a problem now?"

Tolle says it's impossible to feel troubled when your attention is fully in the Now. You have situations that need to be dealt with or accepted—yes. But only worries about the future or regrets about the past can turn them into personal quagmires.

Skeptics may argue that altering your thinking doesn't change the problem, just your perception of it. But that's the magic of it. Higher awareness is often the prelude to a solution.

Tolle says, "Accept—then act. Whatever the present moment contains, accept it as if you had chosen it. Always work with it, not against it. Make it your friend and ally, not your enemy. This will miraculously transform your whole life."

How do you get started? Ironically, by becoming conscious of your lack of consciousness—something the majority of us never do—you take the first step toward an elevated state of mind. Your ability to enjoy your life, and deal successfully with your problems, increases the moment you become fully present.

Beware though. Living in the present moment means abandoning your old ways of thinking. In the present moment there is no judging, cherishing your opinions, or nurturing discontent.

It means slowing down. Relaxing. Focusing on your breath. Listening to the breeze. Or just taking a good look around.

You have the opportunity to enhance your life simply by choosing where to direct your attention. Where should that be?

Right here. Right now. ■

Six Steps to a More Relaxed Life

Many of us lead hectic lives, feeling pressured, harried, or overwhelmed by responsibilities and deadlines.

In his book *The Secret Pulse of Time*, Stefan Klein argues that the culprit is modern society itself. The pace of life has accelerated over the past few decades,—and we are faced with almost limitless opportunities, making it tough to decide how to best spend our time.

Klein recommends six steps to avoid being a slave to the clock, regain control of your time, and live a more relaxed life:

1. Take sovereignty over your time. Many of us have a tendency to load up our schedules unnecessarily. For example, studies show that faced with a choice between a bigger paycheck and more free time, most people go for the money. When we get home from work, many of us are still taking business calls or checking our email. Yet much of this work is unessential or can wait until the next day.

   If you find you don't have time to relax, the first step is to break out of your routine. Plan your days—and weeks—more effectively. Set boundaries between work and home. Change what you're doing.

2. Live in harmony with your biological clock. Our genes determine whether we are early birds or night owls. I know I do my best work in the morning, for example. If I get

waylaid early in the day by non-work-related activities, it takes me twice as long to meet my deadlines in the late afternoon or evening.

Psychologists say you can accomplish more in less time, and make fewer mistakes, by conforming your daily routine to your circadian rhythm.

3. Cultivate leisure time. The world seems to be made up of two types of people, those who must be goaded to work and those who need to be reminded to stop. The latter often develop the unconscious habit of believing that an hour without anything accomplished is an hour wasted.

   But we all need to relax to achieve some balance. As Klein writes, "Two hours at a café without a cell phone, travel, a stroll, music, gardening, the almost forgotten art of conversation—all of these are occasions to modify the pace of life. Leisure does not simply happen when there is a lull in our crowded schedule. We have to create it actively."

4. Experience the moments. We all spend the majority of our time thinking about the future or reminiscing about the past rather than lingering in the present moment. It's a tough habit to break. But the present moment is all we have . . . or ever will have.

   Our resistance to this notion is partly cultural. In the West, we tend to think in terms of efficiency and productivity. It's different in the East. The Japanese tea ceremony, for example, exists so that participants can calm down and sharpen their senses, leaving their worries and responsibilities at the door. It is a reminder that life isn't just a race against time.

   Vietnamese monk and Nobel Peace Prize nominee Thich Nhat Hahn says, "We are very good at preparing to live, but not very good at living. We know how to sacrifice ten years for a diploma, and we are willing to work very hard to get a job, a car, a house and so on. But we have difficulty remembering that we are alive in the present moment, the only moment there is for us to be alive."

5. Learn to concentrate. Americans are famous for doing two things at once. We answer our email while listening to a conference call. We watch TV while having lunch. We drive down the road, listening to the radio, nattering to the kids in the back seat and talking on the cell phone at the same time.

   We think we're multitasking. But are we really doing any of these tasks well? Every time you turn your attention from one problem to another, you interrupt your train of thought. Important information vanishes from your working memory. Most of us can do better work in less time by concentrating on the most important task at hand and eliminating distractions.

6. Set your priorities. Life is mostly about making good choices. Do you want to be the best production manager or the best father? Do you want to earn a higher income or spend more time playing tennis and getting in shape? It's tough to excel in one area without giving short shrift to others.

Only you can decide what is most important. You may be happier working at a Red Cross event than a corporate function. Or spending time with your family rather than chasing that promotion. (After all, it won't be your boss and co-workers weeping when you're gone.)

Your life revolves around the calendar and the clock. But they shouldn't dictate it.

Studies show that continual time pressures create stress—and chronic stress affects your quality of life, undermines your health and lowers your life expectancy.

The key is to slow down, prioritize your activities, and appreciate the many people and blessings that surround you.

As Henry Van Dyke said, "Time is too slow for those who wait, too swift for those who fear, too long for those who grieve, too short for those who rejoice, but for those who love, time is eternity." ∎

ONE OF THE BEST SECRETS OF LIFE

As a young man, I was a devotee of Ayn Rand.

Reading her philosophical novels *Atlas Shrugged* and *The Fountainhead* strengthened my belief in free markets, individual liberty, personal integrity, and the inspirational power of great art.

In particular, Rand's radical independence—she swore that she would never live her life for the sake of another person—seemed downright heroic.

It will come as no surprise, however, that Rand was childless. She also had a reputation for being ill-tempered and egotistical. And she bore grudges. ("She wanted me *dead*," her former paramour Nathaniel Branden told me over dinner one night.)

Hmm. Perhaps there are other role models . . . better ones.

In *Soul Food*, Jack Kornfield and Christina Feldman tell the story of an Illinois family whose daughter became ill and was diagnosed with a life-threatening blood disease.

A search went out for a compatible blood donor but none could be found. Then it was discovered that her 6-year-old brother shared her blood type. The boy's mother and doctor sat down with him to ask if he would be willing to donate blood to save the life of his sister.

To their surprise, he did not answer right away. He needed some time to think about it. After a few days, he came back to his mother and announced he would do it.

As Kornfield and Feldman write, "The following day the doctor brought both children to his clinic and placed them on cots next to each other. He wanted them to see how one was helping the other. First he drew a half pint of blood from the young boy's arm. Then he moved it over to his sister's cot and inserted the needle so her brother could see the effect. In a few minutes color began to pour back into her cheeks.

"Then the boy motioned for the doctor to come over. He wanted to ask a question, very quietly.

" 'Will I start to die right away?' he asked.

You see, when he had been asked to donate his blood to save his sister's life, his 6-year-old mind understood the process literally."

He believed he was trading his life for his sister's. No wonder he needed a few days to mull it over.

In today's society, selflessness is often regarded as naïve or idealistic, an outdated concept promoted by busybodies and do-gooders.

But those who focus solely on themselves have their own set of problems. For starters, many of them don't look terribly happy.

Psychologist Martin Seligman writes that "one of the major symptoms of depression is self-absorption. The depressed person thinks about how she feels a great deal, excessively so. . . . When she detects sadness, she ruminates about it, projecting it into the future and across all her activities, and this in turn increases her sadness."

This is generally beyond the control of someone clinically depressed. Yet cognitive therapists have found that a regimen of goal setting and thought modification is more effective with some patients than antidepressants. The objective is to get the patient looking upward and outward rather than obsessively inward.

Not a bad idea for the rest of us, either. As author Henry Miller said, "Develop interest in life as you see it, in people, things, literature, music—the world is so rich, simply throbbing with rich treasures, beautiful souls and interesting people. Forget yourself."

This is no easy task. From infancy we are programmed to think about *our* wants, *our* needs, *our* feelings, *our* objectives.

This is natural. But it can also be problematic—and embarrassing. When we get all wrapped up in ourselves, we make a pretty small package. We also risk becoming a crashing bore.

Ambrose Bierce captured this sentiment with perfect irony when he defined an egotist as "a person of low taste—more interested in himself than me."

To a certain extent, we are all held captive by our egos. Yet the sages have always taught us how to break free:

Taoism suggests we extend our help without seeking reward. Buddha said that contentment is found in a generous heart, kind speech, and a life of service and compassion. The New Testament tells us it is more blessed to give than to receive.

Many secular philosophers agree. In *Breaking the Spell,* Daniel Dennett writes:

> One of the best secrets of life: let your *self* go. If you can approach the world's complexities, both its glories and its horrors, with an attitude of humble curiosity, acknowledging that however deeply you have seen, you have only just scratched the surface, you will find worlds within worlds, beauties you could not heretofore imagine, and your own mundane preoccupations will shrink to *proper* size . . . for if you can stay centered, and engaged, you will find the hard choices easier, the right words will come to you when you need them, and you will indeed be a better person.

■

THIS VIEW OF LIFE

In 2009 we celebrate both the 200th birthday of Charles Darwin and the 150th anniversary of his masterwork *On the Origin of Species.*

Celebrate, however, is too strong a word in some quarters.

A friend who was raised in a strict fundamentalist household tells me he was brought up to believe Darwin was Beelzebub himself, a bomb-thrower, an atheist who tries to tempt us away from traditional morality and purposeful living.

The truth, as is often the case, is more complicated. Charles Darwin was anything but a firebrand.

Although he had a passion for natural science, Darwin trained at Cambridge to enter the Anglican ministry. He was diverted, however, when he was offered the opportunity to sail to South America as a naturalist aboard the HMS *Beagle.*

He spent the next five years collecting fossils and examining various plant and animal species, particularly in geographically isolated environments like the Galapagos Islands. By the time he returned home, he had formulated most of his theory of evolution by natural selection.

Yet he was reluctant to publish his findings. Aware that his research would shock Victorian society—and his devout wife Emma—he sat on his theory for over a decade, publishing his work only when he learned he was about to be scooped by his contemporary Alfred Russel Wallace.

When it was finally published in November 1859, *On the Origin of Species* was an immediate sensation. The entire stock of 1,250 copies sold out the first day. It has never been out of print.

Yet 150 years later, the book remains controversial. Evolution by natural selection provides a scientific explanation for the diversity of life on earth. Scientists call it the unifying principle of biology.

Yet some religious leaders claim that Darwinism undermines morality and our place in the universe. That it deprives our lives of purpose and meaning. This view is evolving too, however.

Pope John Paul II shocked many followers in 1996 when he proclaimed evolution "more than just a hypothesis" and declared it compatible with Christian faith.

Dr. Francis Collins, a Christian and the scientist who oversaw the Human Genome Project, insists there should be no conflict between evolution and modern religious faith. In *The Language of God: A Scientist Present Evidence for Belief*, he argues that truth cannot contradict truth.

In *Thank God for Evolution*, Reverend Michael Dowd writes, "Most people, in my experience, simply don't know that more than 95 percent of the scientists of the world—including scientists who are devoutly religious—agree on the general flow of natural history . . . The fact that our Universe has been transforming along a discernible path for billions of years—the fact that creation was not a one-time event—is of little or no dispute."

Presbyterian minister Henry G. Brinton agrees. He writes, "In the interest of reconciling science and faith, a helpful distinction would be to say that science deals with things and religion deals with words. When scientists perform their experiments, they are making measurements of the physical properties of things, and no words are allowed to change the results of their research. When religious people use words, on the other hand, they are attempting to create new realities by expressing their understandings, experiences and deepest convictions. There is nothing cheap about religious words well used."

Darwin understood this. In his autobiography, he called the morality of the New Testament "beautiful," adding that when a man acts for the good of others he gains "the love of those with whom he lives; and this latter gain undoubtedly is the highest pleasure on earth."

However, Darwin's unorthodox beliefs did create tension in his life. In one of his wife's letters to him, written before their marriage, she implores him to give up his habit of "believing nothing until it is proved."

Darwin called it "a beautiful letter" and wrote on its envelope, "When I am dead, know how many times I have kissed and cried over this."

Throughout his life, Darwin never claimed to be an atheist. In his autobiography, he wrote, "The mystery of the beginning of all things is insoluble by us; and I for one must be content to remain an Agnostic."

Scientific theory alone did not undermine his faith. Darwin wept uncontrollably at the bedside of his beloved 10-year-old daughter Annie as she was consumed by tuberculosis. Another child died before his second birthday.

Aside from the suffering of innocents, Darwin refused to believe that a just and merciful Omnipotence would condemn his deceased father, a kind and freethinking doctor, to eternal damnation.

Throughout his life, Darwin remained a courageous thinker and an assiduous worker. "A man who dares to waste one hour of time," he once wrote, "has not discovered the value of life."

No one can read his words and fail to recognize a character of complete integrity. Darwin was a man driven by the search for truth. This, in itself, is a sort of spiritual practice.

As psychologist Nathaniel Branden writes in *The Art of Living Consciously,* "Whoever continually strives to achieve a clearer and clearer vision of reality and our place in it—whoever is pulled forward by a *passion* for such clarity—is, to that extent, leading a spiritual life."

Paleontologist Niles Eldredge agrees. In his biography *Darwin: Discovering the Tree of Life,* he writes, "One definition of consciousness is the awareness of mortality, and so far as anyone knows we are the only species whose individuals are conscious of their own eventual death. This is quite a price to pay for the fantastic capacity to be aware of one's existence and to have the privilege of trying to make sense of the world—and of life—while we are here."

As much as any naturalist or philosopher, Darwin helped us understand our selves, our world, and our place in it.

Today he ranks among history's greatest scientists, alongside Copernicus, Newton, and Einstein. And while he was not shy about putting forward the evidence for his theory, he demonstrated great tact and humility in the way he promoted it.

Still, many today resist his view of life, perhaps because they find it too bleak or too humbling. Others, including Darwin himself, have felt otherwise.

He ends *On the Origin of Species* with these words:

"There is grandeur in this view of life, with its several powers, having originally been breathed into a few forms or into one; and that, whilst this planet has gone cycling on according to the fixed laws of gravity, from so simple a beginning endless forms most beautiful and most wonderful have been, and are being, evolved."   ∎

WHY I HOPE STEVE JOBS IS WRONG

A small part of my stock portfolio is invested in companies that I love so much—and patronize so regularly—that I will probably never sell them.

One of those companies is Apple. My shares are up more than 30-fold, even after the recent sell-off. Of course, I've had them a long time. (I bought them before there was an iMac, an iPod, an iPhone, or an iTunes store.)

I credit a lot of my success to CEO Steve Jobs. A visionary business leader, he consistently turns out well-designed, great-looking products that are not only fun to own but look like they belong in the Museum of Modern Art.

Over the years, I've learned to listen when Steve Job speaks. Still, I hope he's wrong this time . . .

When asked at a recent press conference whether Apple intends to market a product to compete with Amazon's Kindle—an electronic reader—he dismissed the idea with a wave of his hand.

"It doesn't matter how good or bad the product is, the fact is that people don't read anymore. . . . The whole product is flawed at the top because people don't read anymore."

What a depressing notion, if true. Reading is our connection to the best thinkers and wisest souls who ever lived. Is it possible to know this and still not read? Can people really prefer to spend their lives wallowing in unthought?

Apparently so.

According to A. C. Nielsen, the average American watches more than 4 hours of TV each day. That's 28 hours a week, or 2 months of nonstop TV watching per year. In a 65-year life, that person will have spent 9 years glued to the tube.

Pretty sad.

Of course, this aversion to serious reading is nothing new. More than 150 years ago, Henry David Thoreau wrote, "Most people have learned to read to serve a paltry convenience, as they have learned to cipher in order to keep accounts and not be cheated in trade; but of reading as a noble, intellectual exercise they know little or nothing."

This is a shame, really. It is through books, chiefly, that we engage with superior minds. People who read regularly think better, speak better, and express themselves more clearly. They understand more and tend to be more interesting.

They are also more likely to be promoted. No single factor correlates more closely with business success than a broad vocabulary. As it turns out, how you dress for work is far less important than how you dress your thoughts.

Wise men have always known this. More than 2,000 years ago, Socrates said, "Employ your time in improving yourself by other men's writing so that you shall come easily by what others have labored hard for."

I think he's right. Of course, I've always been a book man. Always will be. Or as my wife's stepmother once put it, "Were you a nerd as a kid, too?"

I prefer the term bookworm, actually. (Don't ask me the difference.) However, I've always thought the hours I spent reading were a good investment. After all, there simply isn't time to learn *everything* the hard way.

As the Benedictine monk Richard de Bury wrote 700 years ago, "A library of wisdom, is more precious than all wealth, and all things desirable cannot be compared to it."

Except, perhaps, for that new Apple MacBook Pro. I still want one of those.

A RESOLUTION
WORTH KEEPING

A sign in front of a church down the street says, "Resolutions go in one year and out the other."

How true. The other day I was cleaning out my desk and found a list of New Year's resolutions for 2006. Turns out I still haven't lost those pounds, taken that trip, read those books, or updated my estate plan, among other things.

This is when we generally fall back on that ironclad, all-purpose excuse: But I've been so *busy*.

Maybe that's the problem. We spend too much time on things that are urgent but unimportant and not enough on things that are less urgent but more important.

Phone calls, emails, junk mail, and Monday Night Football are urgent. They require our immediate attention, if only to pass on them. Deciding whether to change jobs, end a broken relationship, or what to do with the rest of your life can always wait. Tomorrow is as good as today.

Yet few things are more dispiriting than realizing you're bogged down doing things that don't really matter. As Stephen Covey says, "The main thing is to keep the main thing the main thing."

In his book *First Things First,* he talks about the age-old battle between the clock and the compass. The clock represents your commitments, appointments, schedules, activities—how you manage your time. The compass represents your vision, values, principles, mission, conscience, direction—what you feel is important, how you lead your life.

Where you're headed is so much more important than how fast you're moving. Doing more things faster is no substitute for doing the right things.

Every day we continually make decisions about how we spend our time, from "this afternoon" to "this year." The consequences of those choices determine the quality of our lives.

Yet too often there is a gap between what we're doing and what we know is most important. We want to spend more quality time with the kids. Yet we're off to the mall . . . or to poker night. We know we would look and feel better—and live longer—if we got out and exercised. Yet we plant ourselves like rhubarb in front of ESPN instead.

The result is increased stress—or a gnawing feeling of discontent. Yet there is a solution.

At financial conferences, I often tell attendees that investment success does not come from following the right *predictions*. It comes from following the right *principles*.

Warren Buffett, the world's most famous investor, follows the time-tested value principles of his mentor Benjamin Graham. John Templeton, the man *Money* magazine called "arguably the greatest global stock picker of the century," formulated his own "22 Principles for Successful Investing."

Principles are not ephemeral. They don't come in or out of fashion. (Or shouldn't.) They are timeless and universal. They are markers that provide direction in both good times and bad.

And just as surely as the best investment principles can safeguard our portfolios, the great human principles ought to inspire our behavior.

As Stephen Covey writes in *Everyday Greatness*, "Principles such as *vision, innovation, humility, quality, empathy, magnanimity, perseverance,* and *balance* can mobilize us toward greater personal effectiveness and increased life satisfaction. If you doubt this, consider living life based on their opposites, such as lack of vision, laziness, sloppiness, closed mindedness, revenge, lack of determination, or imbalance. Hardly the ingredients for success."

The challenge is to examine your life and see if your actions are in harmony with your values, with universal principles. How are you treating people? What are you contributing on a daily basis? Are you doing *good* . . . or are you just doing *well*?

How you answer those questions will determine your real success . . . and how you're remembered many years after you're gone.   ■

A THORN WITH
EVERY ROSE

I recently spoke at an investment conference at the Grove Park Inn, a historic hotel on the western slope of Sunset Mountain near Asheville, N.C.

Passing the enormous hearth in the lobby, I noticed an engraving on one of the stones. It was a quatrain written by Frank L. Stanton, a columnist for the *Atlanta Constitution* in the 1890s:

This old world we're livin' in
Is mighty hard to beat
We get a thorn with every rose
But ain't the roses sweet

This was once the most widely quoted poem in the country. But no longer.

According to a 2008 *CBS News/New York* Times poll, Americans' views on the general state of the country hit an all-time low, with 81 percent saying the prospects for the United States are declining, the worst-ever number for this barometer.

Some will argue this just reflected the economic slowdown or the monumental unpopularity of former President Bush. But pollsters report that, for decades now, large percentages have said the country is going downhill, life is getting tougher, our children face a declining future, and the world, in general, is going to hell in a hand basket.

Clearly, we do have serious problems. There is the threat of nuclear proliferation, the specter of terrorism, and the unpleasant fact that our troops are bogged down overseas.

From an economic perspective, the federal deficit keeps ballooning, home prices are falling, the currency is weak, credit is tight, and stock market investors have suffered a brutal bear market.

No wonder Americans are in a foul mood. Especially if this perspective, one that is repeated endlessly by the national media, accurately represents the big picture.

But it doesn't.

The media delivers the world through a highly distorted lens. It doesn't report buildings that don't burn, planes that don't crash, or companies that are hiring instead of laying off.

Our lot has been getting generally better over the years, not worse.

As Gregg Easterbrook of the Brookings Institution recently wrote in the *Wall Street Journal,* "Living standards are the highest they have ever been, including the living standards for the middle class and the poor. All forms of pollution other than greenhouse gases are in decline; cancer, heart disease and stroke incidence are declining; crime is in a long-term cycle of significant decline, and education levels are at all-time highs."

Despite the gloomy headlines, most of us have it pretty darn good.

Consider that in the first half of the 20th century, most people earned a subsistence living through long hours of backbreaking work on farms or in factories.

In 1850, the average workweek was 64 hours. In 1900, it was 53. Today it is 42 hours. On the whole, Americans work less, have more purchasing power, enjoy goods and services in almost unlimited supply, and have much more leisure.

In the first half of our nation's history, most Americans lived and died within a few miles of where they were born. Nothing traveled faster than a horse and, as far as they knew, nothing ever would. Today we have instantaneous global communication, 24-hour broadband Internet access, and same-day travel to distant cities.

Formal discrimination against women and minorities has ended. There is mass home ownership, with central heat and air-conditioning and endless labor-saving devices: stoves, ovens, refrigerators, dishwashers, microwaves, and computers.

Medicine was almost nonexistent 80 years ago. In 1927, for example, President Calvin Coolidge's 16-year-old son Calvin Jr. developed a blister playing tennis without socks at the White House. It became infected. Five days later, he died. Before the advent of antibiotics, tragedies like these were routine.

Advances in medicine and technology have eliminated most of history's plagues. There has been a stunning reduction in infectious diseases.

We complain about the rising cost of health care. But that's only because we routinely live long enough to depend on it. The average American lifespan has almost doubled over the past century.

Today we enjoy economic and political freedoms denied to billions around the world and throughout history. We live long lives, in good health and in comfortable circumstances. By almost any measure, we are living better than 99.9 percent of those who came before us.

Yet we routinely tell pollsters that life is hard and things are getting steadily worse.

It's time to take the larger view. If we don't, we risk becoming the mopey character Steve Martin portrays when he mumbles, "The only joy I know is a dishwashing liquid."

As Easterbrook writes in *The Progress Paradox*:

> Perhaps Western society has lost its way, producing material goods in impressive superfluity but also generating so much stress and pressure that people cannot enjoy what they attain. Perhaps men and women must reexamine their priorities demanding less, caring more about each other, appreciating what they have rather than grousing about what they do not have, giving more than lip service to the wisdom that money cannot buy happiness.

How do we do this? We can re-order our lives so that they are less hectic, less stressful.

We all have problems. But as author Robert Ringer used to say, whatever your troubles, the odds are small that anyone is going to throw you up against a wall and pull out a machine gun. We can start improving the quality of our lives simply by changing our perspective.

And we can accept that if something is missing in our lives, it is probably a sense of gratitude, not material possessions.

Take a moment to appreciate your incredible good fortune just to be alive. As Oxford biologist Richard Dawkins writes in *Unweaving the Rainbow*:

> We are going to die, and that makes us the lucky ones. Most people are never going to die because they are never going to be born. The potential people who could have been here in my place but who will in fact never see the light of day outnumber the sand grains of Sahara. Certainly those unborn ghosts include greater poets than Keats, scientists greater than Newton. We know this because the set of possible people allowed by our DNA so massively outnumbers the set of actual people. In the teeth of these stupefying odds it is you and I, in our ordinariness, that are here.

True, it's not a perfect world. But it's the only one we've got. And we're only here once.

As my Dad used to say, "If you work it right, once is enough." ∎

■ THE BEST WAY OUT

Last year, I suffered a home invasion.

Twenty-two of my relatives showed up for Thanksgiving. (Some of them invited.)

We gathered to give thanks for our health, our friends, our family . . . and a twenty-six-pound bird stuffed with cornbread dressing and surrounded by cranberry sauce, squash soufflé, parmesan-garlic green beans with almonds, and sweet potato casserole.

(No wonder the pilgrims had the Wampanoag tribe over.)

With all our blessings, however, is one day of thanks ever enough?

Of course not. In his book *Discovering the Laws of Life*, the famed money manager and philanthropist John Templeton recommended a different approach. He called it *thanksliving*.

Thanksliving means practicing an attitude of perpetual gratitude.

That's not hard when times are good. But for many, it's tough out there right now. The economy is sputtering. The job market is weak. Credit is tight.

Combine these with the real estate slump and the recent swoon in stock and bond markets and an attitude of continual thankfulness becomes a tall order.

Yet Templeton offers a radical solution. Don't just give thanks for your blessings. Be grateful for your problems, too.

This seems wildly counterintuitive at first blush. But facing up to our challenges makes us stronger, smarter, tougher, and more valuable as parents, mates, employees . . . and human beings.

Solving problems is what we're made for. It's what makes life worth living.

"Adversity, when overcome, strengthens us," says Templeton. "So we are giving thanks not for the problem itself but for the strength and knowledge that will come from it. Giving thanks for this growth ahead of time will help you to grow through—not just go through—your challenges."

Circumstances alone never decide our fate. We all have the ability to shape our destiny. And it begins with believing we can.

Worries, regrets, and complaints solve nothing. They change nothing. Rather they undermine your health, your social environment, and your quality of life.

Difficult situations are rarely resolved with positive thoughts or gratitude alone, however. It takes another crucial ingredient: sustained action.

Even then, some problems are intractable. Others—like the death of a loved one—are insoluble. In certain circumstances, only an attitude of acceptance moves us forward.

Most of our day-to-day problems, however, are created by the person in the mirror.

We made them. And we can fix them.

According to Unitarian pastor Preston Bradley, "The world has a way of giving what is demanded of it. If you are frightened and look for failure and poverty, you will get them, no matter how hard you may try to succeed. Lack of faith in yourself, in what life will do for you, cuts you off from the good things in the world. Expect victory and make victory. Nowhere is this truer than in the business of life, where bravery and faith bring both material and spiritual rewards."

This lesson is best learned at an early age. Once when I was about seven years old, my father asked me to load some big, heavy-looking boxes into his car.

I looked them over doubtfully. "I can't," I said.

It was one of the few times I've ever seen him angry. "What was that word you just used?" he demanded.

"Can't?" I asked, sheepish.

"I don't ever want to hear you use that word again." Then he strode off as I (ahem) loaded the boxes.

Journalist Sam Levenson had a similar experience:

"It was on my fifth birthday that Papa put his hand on my shoulder and said, 'Remember, my son, if you ever need a helping hand, you'll find one at the end of your arm.'"

I'm not suggesting it's wrong to ask for help. Under certain circumstances, you won't succeed without it. We could all use a boost from time to time.

But it's much more satisfying—and dignifying—when we solve our problems ourselves.

In addition to showing us what we're made of, working through our setbacks makes us more sensitive to—and more compassionate toward—the problems of our fellowman.

Look around and you'll see plenty of good people with more troubles than you. And the true spirit of thanksliving means remembering—and giving—all year round.

Whatever problems you're grappling with—personal, social, or financial—the best course is to face them with all the courage, patience, and equanimity you can muster.

And, if possible, be grateful. Opportunity often shows up disguised as hard work.

On occasion, of course, our problems are simply bigger than we are. In an address in 1859, Abraham Lincoln recounted the tale of King Solomon:

> It is said that an Eastern monarch once charged his wise men to invent him a sentence, to be ever in view, and which should be true and appropriate in all times and situations. They presented him with the words: "And this, too, shall pass away." How much it expresses! How chastening in the hour of pride! How consoling in the depths of affliction!

That's something worth keeping in mind.

Whatever your problems, few of them can withstand the onslaught of optimism, persistence, and a genuine spirit of gratitude. So get moving.

As the poet Robert Frost reminds us, "The best way out is always through." ■

PART THREE

ATTITUDES AND GRATITUDE

There may be such a thing as a born salesman. If so, I wasn't one of them.

As a kid, I was shy. As a young adult, introverted. As a newly minted salesman in my first job out of college, an abject failure.

Rather than firing me, my manager, perhaps in desperation, bought me a ticket to see a professional motivator, a nerdy, middle-aged guy with a funny name, Zig Ziglar. During his performance—and it was definitely a performance—I remember thinking I'd never seen an "old guy" with that much energy and enthusiasm. I left feeling so good—about life, the future, the whole world—that I wasn't sure what to do with myself.

So much of what we hear every day is trivial or mundane, listening to an inspirational speaker can be truly elevating.

The next morning, however, a strange feeling settled in. I remembered the positive energy and the emotional lift from the previous day, but I couldn't recall many of the specifics of what he'd actually said. (It might have helped if I'd taken a pencil.)

But he did make one statement I couldn't forget: "It's your attitude, not your aptitude, that determines your altitude." That sounded hokey to me then. It still does today. (Hokey is what the truth becomes when it's been hanging around forever.)

As a young man, I doubt that I realized just how important those words are, how essential. No matter how much talent or money you have, people judge you by your attitude. An inexperienced worker with a great attitude is a potential asset to any company. An experienced worker with a bad attitude is a cancer that can negatively affect everyone around her. Employers may initially feel that these talented people with their noses bent out of joint are too valuable to let go. More often than not, they discover that their business is too valuable to keep them on.

No matter what you're trying to achieve in business, education, sports, or love, your attitude can be your greatest asset—or a huge liability. Fortunately, this factor is under your control.

We have great examples in men like Randy Pausch and Viktor Frankl. Mihaly Csikszentmihalyi teaches us about "optimal experience." Hamilton Jordan reminds us why "there's no such thing as a bad day." And Robert Frost shows us "the best way out" of the thorniest situations.

In life, your attitude is your most potent weapon. And your shield? A genuine sense of gratitude.

WHAT MATTERS MOST

At Thanksgiving, Anne, a family friend, looked and sounded great.

Today she is dying of cancer. In the last few weeks she has lost her eyesight. Half her face is paralyzed. And she has refused more chemo, describing the results of last week's MRI as "just horrible."

When I walked into Hallmark, I told the clerk I was looking for a special kind of card.

"It's for someone who isn't well," I said. "And she knows she isn't going to get better."

The clerk nodded, said she knew just what I needed and led me to a special section with headings like "Hope," "Strength," and "Serious Illness."

Standing there reading the messages in those cards, thinking of all the grief-stricken people out there selecting them—or (worse) receiving them—is enough to make you weep. I finally settled on *"May you gather strength from the love of those around you,"* scrawled a note about how I'd love to stop in if she felt like visitors, and dropped it in the mailbox.

When he began teaching at Cornell, the Russian novelist Vladimir Nabokov said he knew just two things: One, life is beautiful, and two, life is sad. The reason life is sad, in part, is because it's going to end.

Yet death, our most unwelcome guest, can also do us a favor. It can remind us, the mourners, what's most important.

As Jack Kerouac observed, "Pondering on death, with or without wine—brings enlightenment."

Too many of us spend our days moving with the hustling crowd, mindlessly doing more or less what everyone else is doing, acting like we have all the time in the world. That is, until we get a wake-up call and learn that someone close to us has had a bad accident or is suddenly very ill.

Increased awareness of our own mortality needn't lead to fear and anxiety, however. We can use it as an opportunity to answer the question posed by poet Mary Oliver, "Tell me what is it you plan to do with your one wild and precious life?"

Do you know? Or are you so consumed with projects, deadlines, and responsibilities that you haven't given it much thought lately?

Meanwhile, the clock is ticking. And this realization is a good thing.

Viewed from the prospect of eternity, we are really no more durable than the mayfly. Some of us spend our time just as frivolously. Others are bored. As author Susan Ertz quipped, "Millions long for immortality who don't know what to do with themselves on a rainy Sunday afternoon."

Greek mythology, on the other hand, gives us the story of Tithonus, a Trojan who was granted immortality by the gods but grew to hate his life.

Whatever path he chose, he could always take it later. Whatever options he faced, ultimately he could have them all. Time became meaningless, oppressive even. He lost his ardor for life. In the end, he petitions Zeus to release him from eternity. He begs for mortality so that, once again, *his choices might matter.*

Each of us has been granted an incomparable gift, a brief stay on this little blue ball. How will you spend it? To what end will you use it?

These are the most important question we can ask ourselves. And the answers can be read in the way we live our lives.

"Death is not the greatest loss," Norman Cousins warned. "The greatest loss is what dies inside us while we live."

Doctors generally observe that terminal patients who have truly lived their lives—who have strived and loved and taken risks—generally have an easier time with their dying.

Patients in nursing homes routinely express more regret for the chances they never took than the ones that worked out poorly.

Singer Bono, nominated for the Nobel Peace Prize and granted numerous awards for his activism for world poverty, said in a recent interview, "I'm tired of dreaming. I'm into doing at the moment."

He is someone who has chosen to live life on his own terms and in service to the values that matter to him most. It is unlikely that you or I will ever accomplish as much. But that's okay.

For most of us, born without the immense talents of a da Vinci or Beethoven or Lincoln, the true measure of our lives is not what we achieve—and certainly not what we accumulate—but rather who we are, the number of people we touch, and what is grieved in our absence.

As the novelist E. M. Forster observed, "Death destroys a man, but the idea of death saves him." ■

The Last Human
Freedom

Four years ago, a friend and former colleague was going through a difficult divorce. (Is there any other kind?)

He didn't want to separate from his wife, and he hated being apart from his two young daughters. In the midst of this, he walked into work one day and was suddenly and unceremoniously fired from his job.

That evening he went home and took his own life.

It was a terrible shock to everyone who knew him. And a tragic loss, especially for his girls, who were still in grade school.

I was out of town when I received the call delivering the grim news. I felt awful that I hadn't been there to offer some consolation. Although I don't know what, if anything, I could have done to change his mind. I often imagine I would have simply listened and maybe offered a few words about Viktor Frankl and "the last human freedom."

Born in 1905, Frankl was an Austrian neurologist and psychologist. He was also a Holocaust survivor.

In 1942, Frankl and his wife and parents were deported to the ghetto of Theresienstadt. From there, he was eventually sent to Turkeheim, a concentration camp not far from Dachau. His wife was shipped to the Bergen-Belsen concentration camp, where she died. His mother and father were sent to Auschwitz, where they too were killed.

After three years, Frankl was liberated by American forces in April 1945. He later wrote a world-famous book about his experience, *Man's Search for Meaning.*

In the book, Frankl described the terrible physical and psychological indignities inflicted on him and his fellow inmates in the camps. But he also wrote movingly about a particular form of spiritual heroism—what he called "the last of the human freedoms."

"We who lived in concentration camps can remember the men who walked through the huts comforting others, giving away their last piece of bread. They may have been few in number, but they offer sufficient proof that everything can be taken from a man but one thing: the last of the human freedoms—to choose one's own attitude in any given set of circumstances."

The dignified way these men and women bore their sufferings was a magnificent inner achievement. Few of us will ever deal with circumstances as tragic as those experienced by Frankl and millions of his fellow Jews at the hands of the Nazi regime. Yet Frankl shows us that the attitude we bring to our problems can be an inspiration to others . . . and perhaps even to ourselves.

If you're like me, looking back you often discover that the most difficult circumstances in your life often added the most meaning. Adversity shows us what really matters.

Painful as these times are, they shape us—and help us grow as individuals. As Tom Culve famously said "a calm sea does not produce a skilled sailor. We cannot direct the wind, but we can adjust the sails."

This is not just a matter of thinking positively. Yes, dealing successfully with difficult circumstances is partly about bringing the right attitude to bear. But Frankl also argues that genuine spirituality is not merely the product of right thinking or meditation. It comes from right action. And he offers us a general guideline: "Live as if you were living already for the second time and as if you had acted the first time as wrongly as you are about to act now." Frankl calls this emphasis on both attitude and responsibility "the categorical imperative."

Following it isn't always easy. Occasionally, life hands us circumstances so dire that nothing practical can be done. (Think of a loved one with a terminal illness.) Sometimes the best we can do is simply play the hand we're dealt.

Still, it is *our choice* how we play it.

As Frankl writes, "We must never forget that we may also find meaning in life even when confronted with a hopeless situation, when facing a fate that cannot be changed. For what then matters is to bear witness to the uniquely human potential at its best, which is to transform a personal tragedy into a triumph, to turn one's predicament into a human achievement. When we are no longer able to change a situation . . . we are challenged to change ourselves." ■

WHY YOU SHOULD THINK
BEFORE YOU "BLINK"

In the bestseller *Blink: The Power of Thinking Without Thinking,* author Malcolm Gladwell points out that our "adaptive unconscious" is constantly making assessments about people and situations in just a matter of seconds.

He argues that these snap judgments are not just good, but extraordinary. For example, he cites a study showing that college students can watch short film clips of professors lecturing and rate them as accurately as students who spend an entire term with them, even when the clips are only two seconds long. (Two seconds!)

This is quirky and interesting, but I'm skeptical. Much of my own experience has been a rebuttal to this line of thinking.

How many times have you made a new acquaintance, thought you knew him, and then one day discovered he was not the person you thought he was? How many times have you been badgered, cajoled, or (okay) dragged to an event that turned out to be a lot more fun than you imagined?

In making snap judgments, we often shortchange our friends, our family, our co-workers, even ourselves. We miss the opportunity for new experiences and relationships. And, more often than not, we are completely unaware of it.

Investment legend John Templeton once wrote, "A successful life depends less on how long you live than on how much you can pack into the time you have. If you can find a way to make every day an adventure—even if it's only a matter of walking down an unfamiliar street or ordering an untried cut of meat—you will find that your life becomes more productive, richer, and more interesting. You also become more interesting to others."

Yet, as Gladwell points out, we're much more apt to "think without thinking." These instant assessments, however, are not always on target . . .

When I first met my pal Rob Fix at work more than two decades ago, I had two overwhelming impressions. One, he talked too much and, two, he was a bit of a kook. For the first several weeks I knew him, I avoided him like the IRS.

Then at a party at a friend's house one evening, I noticed a crowd of people in the backyard. They were gathered around Rob, who had brought over his Celestron telescope and was busy showing everyone the moon, the planets, the Orion Nebula, and the Andromeda Galaxy.

"How far is it to the moon, anyway?" asked a young woman who was peering into the telescope.

"Now let me see," said Rob, thinking out loud. "I just drove it the other day . . ."

Hey, I remember thinking to myself, this guy isn't so bad. He's actually pretty funny.

Of course, now that I've known him for 26 years I realize that my first impression of Rob was totally off base. He's not a guy who talks too much and is a bit of a kook. He's a guy who talks *way* too much and is the biggest kook I've ever met. He is, in fact, the world's most lovable kook. Perhaps that's why he was the best man at my wedding.

Yes, our prejudgments can mislead us . . .

A friend declines tickets to a jazz concert because he *knows* he wouldn't like it. My daughter Hannah turns up her nose at every food she doesn't recognize. (Not to mention the vast majority she does.) We pass on the weekend trip away because we imagine "it's too much of a hassle."

Each day we face dozens of small decisions. For expediency, if nothing else, we lapse into the safe, the familiar, the unthinking—denying ourselves the pleasure of a new discovery.

Just ask Walker Percy. In his foreword to John Kennedy Toole's *A Confederacy of Dunces,* he describes how the book came to his attention:

> While I was a teaching at Loyola in 1976 I began to get telephone calls from a lady unknown to me. What she proposed was pre-posterous. It was not that she had written a couple of chapters of a novel and wanted to get into my class. It was that her son, who was dead, had written an entire novel during the early sixties, a big novel, and she wanted me to read it. Why would I want to do that? I asked her. Because it was a great novel, she said.
>
> Over the years I have become very good at getting out of things I don't want to do. And if ever there was something I didn't want to do, this was surely it: to deal with the mother of a dead novel-ist and, worst of all, to have to read a manuscript that she said was great, and that, as it turned out, was a badly smeared, scarcely readable carbon.
>
> But the lady was persistent, and it somehow came to pass that she stood in my office handing me the hefty manuscript. There was no getting out of it; only one hope remained—that I could read a few pages and that they would be bad enough for me, in good con-science, to read no farther. Usually I can do just that. Indeed the first paragraph often suffices. My only fear was that this one might be just good enough, so that I would have to keep reading.
>
> In this case I read on. And on. First with the sinking feeling that it was not bad enough to quit, then with a prickle of interest, then a growing excitement, and finally an incredulity: surely it was not possible that it was this good . . .

Oh, it's good all right. His discovery went on to win the Pulitzer Prize for Fiction in 1981 and has since sold more than two million copies. The novel—which features the hilarious mis-adventures of slob extraordinaire Ignatius Reilly—is now regarded as a comic masterpiece.

Let's be grateful that Walker Percy didn't follow his intuition, his instant assessment, his inner "blink." And maybe we should keep a close eye on our own, too.

Life really is full of surprises. But "thinking without thinking" may not be the best way to discover them. ∎

THE MOST STUPID
OF VICES

Economists Sara Solnick and David Hemenway recently conducted a survey where they asked participants if they would rather earn $50,000 a year while other people make $25,000, or earn $100,000 a year while other people get $250,000?

Sit down for this one. The majority of people selected the first option. They would rather make twice as much as others even if that meant earning half as much as they could have.

This is completely nuts, of course. Yet other findings in the study confirmed the envious nature of contemporary culture. People said, for instance, they would rather be average-looking in a community where no one is considered attractive than merely good-looking in the company of stunners.

When it came to education, parents said they would rather have an average child in a crowd of dunces than a smart child in a class full of brilliant students.

What is going on here? In his new book *The Mind of the Market*, *Scientific American* columnist Michael Shermer writes that "Our sense of happiness tends to be based on positional and relative rankings compared to what others have."

There's one problem, however. It doesn't work.

As the philosopher Bertrand Russell pointed out, "Envy consists in seeing things never in themselves, but only in their relations. If you desire glory, you may envy Napoleon, but Napoleon envied

145

Caesar, Caesar envied Alexander, and Alexander, I daresay, envied Hercules, who never existed."

Of all the dissatisfactions we face, surely none is more menial than envy. It denies us contentment, is a waste of time, and is an insult to ourselves. Worst of all, it's completely self-imposed.

"Envy is the most stupid of vices," wrote the novelist Honore de Balzac, "for there is no single advantage to be gained from it."

Face it. We all know people who are smarter, fitter, richer, funnier, more talented, or better looking. But so what?

Thinking this way only keeps you from appreciating your own uniqueness and self-worth, things that, not incidentally, do lead to greater happiness. Especially when combined with a strong sense of purpose.

As Shermer writes, "Feeling ennobled is a pleasurable emotion that arises out of this deepest sense of purpose. Although there are countless activities people engage in to satisfy this deep-seated need, the research shows that there are four means by which we can bootstrap ourselves toward happiness through purposeful action." These include:

1. Deep love and family commitment.
2. Meaningful work and career.
3. Social and political involvement.
4. Transcendency and spirituality.

Note that psychologists have yet to discover the route to happiness by comparing ourselves to others. (Although it never hurts to measure yourself against your own ideals.)

Concentrating on your own fortunes—and improving those of others—is guaranteed to generate more satisfaction than sizing up the Joneses. Besides, if you knew everything the other guy is dealing with, you might prefer your own circumstances anyway. Recall Richard Cory:

Whenever Richard Cory went down town,
We people on the pavement looked at him:

He was a gentleman from sole to crown,
Clean favored, and imperially slim.
And he was always quietly arrayed,
And he was always human when he talked;
But still he fluttered pulses when he said,
"Good-morning," and he glittered when he walked.
And he was rich—yes, richer than a king,
And admirably schooled in every grace:
In fine, we thought that he was everything
To make us wish that we were in his place.
So on we worked, and waited for the light,
And went without the meat, and cursed the bread;
And Richard Cory, one calm summer night,
Went home and put a bullet through his head.

Don't begrudge the other guy his blessings. Instead, count your own.

As Mark Twain observed, "Pity is for the living, envy is for the dead." ■

THE PSYCHOLOGY
OF OPTIMAL EXPERIENCE

We all have troubles. In many ways, they define our lives. But, according to philosopher Abraham Kaplan, we can deal with them more effectively if we recognize them as either problems or predicaments.

The difference? Problems, says Kaplan, can be solved. Predicaments can only be coped with.

If you work in downtown Baltimore, for example, you may be worried about crime. This is a predicament, not a problem. You can install a security system in your car, avoid the worst areas after dark, or arrange a transfer to a different office. But these are coping mechanisms. You are not going to "fix" crime in Baltimore.

A more serious predicament we all face is the occasional death of a loved one.

We can spend time grieving with family and friends, join a support group, or take up new activities to keep our minds from becoming preoccupied. But death itself cannot be bargained with.

Fortunately, most of our troubles are not predicaments, but problems. You may worry, for instance, that you haven't saved enough for a comfortable retirement. If so, you have plenty of company.

According to the 2008 Retirement Confidence Survey by the Employee Benefit Research Institute (EBRI), 36 percent of workers have less than $10,000 in retirement savings. Another 13 percent have less than $25,000.

Clearly, this is a problem, but one with a straightforward solution. You can increase your income. You can spend less. Or you can earn a higher return on your investments. (Doing all three, of course, will get you there quickest.)

Or, you may be one of the millions of Americans who struggles with obesity. If so, it is probably having a detrimental effect on your health, your self-image, and your quality of life.

For some of us, this is both a problem and a predicament. After all, genetics determine your basic body type. As you learned in fifth-grade health, you were born an ectomorph, a mesomorph, or an endomorph. You cannot change this.

But anyone can eat better, exercise more, or both. Not easy, but there *is* a solution.

Why is it important to label the trials you face either problems or predicaments?

According to John C. Maxwell, author of *The Difference Maker,* "When people treat a predicament as a problem, they become frustrated, angry, or depressed. They waste energy. They make bad decisions. And when people treat problems as predicaments, they often settle, give up, or see themselves as victims."

Understand this and you've taken the first step toward dealing with your predicaments and solving your problems.

Nielsen Media Research tells us that Americans love reality shows where contestants are put in high-pressure situations and challenged to "win" using every bit of intelligence, cunning, and resourcefulness they can muster.

Why not view your own problems the same way? If you have a boring job, an inattentive spouse, or a looming financial setback, why not use all your smarts, imagination, and creativity to turn the tables?

My guess is that if you were in front of a national television audience—and in danger of being voted off the show—you'd come up with something pretty good, something that would surprise the people around you.

In fact, this is exactly what you *should* be doing, according to Mihaly Csikszentmihalyi, author of *Flow: The Psychology of Optimal*

Experience. He argues that the quickest way to increase your life satisfaction is to quit seeing your problems as difficulties and start viewing them as an enjoyable challenge.

(He isn't the first to articulate this notion, incidentally. For centuries, Buddhists have embraced difficult people and situations as opportunities for spiritual development. Without them, what chance do you have to practice compassion, tolerance, or forgiveness?)

Facing your problems this way requires just two things: a bit of imagination and a positive attitude. The payoff, in turn, can be huge. Whether you want to start your own business, lose 30 pounds, or get out of debt, you can begin by relishing the challenge.

You might surprise yourself, too. Not only by achieving your goals, but by seeing how much satisfaction you get just moving toward them in a disciplined way.

Think of it as your own reality show. (One that, ironically, actually *deals* with reality.) The obstacles in front of you give you the opportunity to show the world—and yourself—what you're made of.

Just remember that your predicaments require interpretive thinking and must be endured. Your problems require analytic thinking—and cannot withstand the sustained assault of creative thinking and positive action.

So why not attack yours today with a fresh mindset and a new attitude? You have nothing to lose but your troubles.   ■

THE COURAGE
OF RANDY PAUSCH

Courage means different things to different people.

Hemingway called it "grace under pressure." The writer Anais Nin said, "Life shrinks or expands in proportion to one's courage." Winston Churchill called it the greatest virtue "and the guarantor of all the others."

There are different types of courage, of course. There is the heroic courage U.S. soldiers demonstrated when they spilled onto the beach at Normandy in June 1944. Or when New York City firefighters rushed into the World Trade Center on 9/11.

Then there is everyday courage. The kind it takes to experiment with your own life, whether falling in love, changing careers, or bearing up under difficult circumstances.

Americans talk about courage a lot. We idolize it many ways, as all free people should. But we seldom have the opportunity to witness great courage firsthand.

However, millions of Americans did when they watched "The Last Lecture" by Randy Pausch, a young Professor of Computer Science at Carnegie Mellon University (CMU) in Pittsburgh.

Randy's story is well known. In September 2006, he was diagnosed with metastatic pancreatic cancer. This diagnosis, as you may know, is essentially a death sentence—and an especially tragic one when, like Randy, you are 46 years old with three small children.

Although he pursued an aggressive treatment that included major surgery and experimental chemotherapy, by August 2007 the disease had metastasized to his liver and spleen. He was told he had three months to live.

On September 18, 2007, Randy delivered a talk entitled "Really Achieving Your Childhood Dreams."

In a last lecture, an academic is generally asked to think deeply about what matters most and then give a hypothetical "final talk" on a topic such as "what wisdom would you try to impart to the world if you knew it was your last chance."

In Randy's case, the talk was anything but hypothetical. He used it as an opportunity to talk about things he held dear: the importance of dreams, how to achieve yours, and how to help others achieve theirs.

However, the lecture was actually an artifice. The people in attendance thought Randy was giving an academic lecture. But it was a ruse. The lecture was filmed to give him an opportunity to tell his three young kids the things he would like to tell them growing up . . . if only he were going to be there to do it.

The lecture is truly inspiring. To watch, visit www.youtube .com/watch?v=ji5_MqicxSo

(If you don't have a lump in your throat by the end, be sure to have someone check your pulse.)

The confederate colonel Robert G. Ingersoll once said, "The greatest test of courage on earth is to bear defeat without losing heart."

Randy Pausch provided a living testimonial. Sadly, he lost his battle with pancreatic cancer on July 25, 2008.   ■

ARE YOU READY FOR THE 21-DAY CHALLENGE?

Would you like to enjoy better health, have a more satisfying job, feel less pain, experience less conflict in your relationships, and live in peace and contentment?

In a matter of weeks—time that will pass anyway—you can have the life you've always dreamed of living. You only have to do one thing.

Stop complaining.

Face it. We all do it. The weather is lousy. The price is outrageous. The kids are slobs. The boss is a jerk. The freeway's a mess. And so on.

Most of us feel that when we're complaining we're just speaking our minds. Except something else is going on here, too. When we complain we are focusing on what is wrong with our lives instead of what's right.

Studies show that our motives aren't always the best, either.

When we point out other people's faults, for example, psychologists say it's often a thinly veiled way of suggesting that we are better than they are. We build ourselves up by tearing others down. People with a healthy self-esteem don't need to do this.

Those who complain about the quality of the food or wine at a restaurant are sometimes striving to create an impression of sophistication or discrimination. But it backfires. You ruin your companion's meal and look supercilious at the same time.

153

Bear in mind, "My steak is overcooked" is a fact, not a complaint. "I wouldn't feed this to my dog" . . . well, you be the judge.

We also use complaints as excuses. In his new book *A Complaint Free World,* Reverend Will Bowen writes, "If you are saying things like 'Men are commitment-phobic,' 'Everyone in my family is fat,' 'I'm not coordinated,' 'My father told me I'd never amount to anything,' you are making yourself a victim. Victims don't become victors. And you get to choose which you will be."

Bowen says it's fine to use terms like "Of course!," "Wouldn't you know it?," "Just my luck!," and "This always happens to me!," but only when something good happens. Never miss an opportunity to say "Of course" when something goes well for you, no matter how small.

There's nothing wrong with expressing dissatisfaction. Dissatisfaction is the mother of progress. The key is how you express yourself. You can bellyache about how bad things are. Or you can motivate those around you by describing how much better things will be when a bad situation is improved.

Realize that you create your life with the words you choose. You can describe something as a problem, or call it an opportunity. You can complain that "I have to . . . ," or you can say "I get to. . . ." A negative turn of events can be described as a "setback," or you can call it a "challenge."

Some folks might argue that carping and complaining each day is normal. But maybe you're better than normal. Maybe you can be exceptional . . . outstanding . . . a positive influence on those around you.

As Reverend Bowen says, "Complaining should happen infrequently; criticism and gossip, never. If we are honest with ourselves, life events that lead us to legitimately complain are exceedingly rare. . . . To be a happy person who has mastered your thoughts and has begun creating your life by design, you need a very high threshold of what leads you to express grief, pain, and discontent."

You are probably better off than Stephen Hawking, for example. As a young man at Cambridge University, he began developing symptoms of Lou Gehrig's disease. As it progressed, he became almost completely physically disabled. Yet he has gone on to produce groundbreaking research in theoretical cosmology and quantum gravity. Today he holds Isaac Newton's chair as the Lucasian Professor of Mathematics at Cambridge.

"It is a waste of time to be angry about my disability," says Hawking. "One has to get on with life and I haven't done badly. People won't have time for you if you are always angry or complaining."

If you need any further incentive, recognize that complaining undermines your health. It creates stress in your life. The more you complain, the more stressful your life becomes. According to *Forbes,* all seven of the top-selling drugs in the United States are for illnesses exacerbated by stress. Americans are so stressed out we spend over $30 billion a year on them.

You may believe you're one of those souls who rarely complains. Or you may feel that complaining is so much a part of your nature that there's nothing you can do about it. Either way, you're probably wrong.

That's why I invite you to take Reverend Bowen's 21-Day Challenge. Try going 21 consecutive days without complaining. (Bowen says it takes 21 days for a new habit to become ingrained.)

Visit his website www.AComplaintFreeWorld.org and order two purple "Complaint Free" bracelets, one for yourself and one for someone you love. (The bracelets are free. There is a shipping charge of 75 cents.)

Begin wearing the bracelet on either wrist. When you catch yourself complaining, gossiping, or criticizing, move the bracelet to the other wrist and begin again. Stay with it until you can go 21 days without a complaint.

This is tougher than it sounds. So far, more than 5 million people have ordered the bracelets. The average person reports needing 4 to 8 months to go a full 21 days without complaining.

But the testimonials are glorious. This simple practice in mindfulness has transformed people's lives and elevated entire organizations.

So order your bracelets. In the meantime, here's an amusing story from Reverend Bowen's book to put you in the right frame of mind:

A young monk joined an order that required total silence. At his discretion, the abbot could allow any monk to speak. It was nearly five years before the abbot approached the novice monk and said, "You may speak two words." Choosing his words carefully, the monk said, "Hard bed." With genuine concern, the abbot said, "I'm sorry your bed isn't comfortable. We'll see if we can get you another one."

Around his tenth year in the monastery, the abbot came to the young monk and said, "You may say two more words." "Cold food," the monk said. "We'll see what we can do," the abbot said.

On the monk's fifteenth anniversary, the abbot said again, "You may now speak two words." "I quit," the monk said. "It's probably for the best," replied the abbot. "You've done nothing but gripe since you got here."

No Such Thing as a Bad Day

Hamilton Jordan passed away last year without much fanfare.

History will remember him as Chief of Staff to President Jimmy Carter and as a high-level advisor to independent Presidential candidate Ross Perot.

But some of us will remember him for other reasons . . .

Jordan was diagnosed with cancer three times. The first was lymphoma, which he believed was a result of his exposure to Agent Orange in Vietnam. That battle was followed by bouts with melanoma and prostate cancer.

Eight years ago, he published *No Such Thing as a Bad Day,* the story of his personal struggles. In an interview with WebMD, he was asked about his choice of title.

"Well," he said, "I was counseling a young man who had a brain tumor, and I called him one day, and I asked him, 'Are you having a good day?' and he said, 'Well, my wife is 32 years old, my kids are 4 and 6, and my doctor tells me I have about two months to live. There's no such thing as a bad day.'"

Jordan was impressed with this attitude and came to embody it himself. Despite surgery and grueling chemotherapy, he used what he called "all my emotional and spiritual resources" to focus on being well, repeatedly telling friends and family he was "just very, very lucky and blessed."

During the course of his journey, Jordan created his "Top Ten Tips for Cancer Patients." Perhaps you know someone you can share them with. Here they are:

1. Be an active partner in the medical decisions that are about your life. Don't be passive. Learn about your disease and participate in the decisions that are made.
2. Seek and know the truth about your illness and prognosis. If you don't have the facts and know the truth, you won't make good decisions.
3. Get a second opinion. Good doctors don't mind that. If yours objects, find another one.
4. Determine upfront how broad or narrow your physician's experience is. You want someone who is very familiar with your disease.
5. If you have a poor prognosis or rare form of cancer, try to get to a center of excellence. (A place like Johns Hopkins, M. D. Anderson, or the Cleveland Clinic, if possible.) Sometimes this is a matter of cost, but insurance generally covers treatments at these centers.
6. Do not allow your caregivers to project their values, goals, and expectations onto you. In his book, Jordan tells the story of a 68-year-old patient who was diagnosed with prostate cancer. His 35-year-old doctor reasoned that since his life expectancy was only five or six years, he should do nothing. The patient rejected the diagnosis and had his prostate removed. Many years later he was still alive and in good health.
7. Understand the economics of cancer care. Let your doctor know what you're willing to do to supplement your coverage to get a good diagnosis. Don't find yourself in a situation where you turn down a $600 test your doctor wants to run because your insurance doesn't cover it.
8. Find a doctor in whom you can place your trust and confidence. If your doctor doesn't believe he or she can cure

you, you won't believe you'll be cured. Find one with a fighting spirit.

9. Treat your mind as well as your body. Get outside. See friends. Stay as active as you can. When you are happy and engaged with life, your immune system is stronger.
10. Your attitude and beliefs are your best weapons against cancer. Your emotional, intellectual, and physical responses to the words "You have cancer" have a lot to do with your survival and quality of life. A positive spirit and the will to live can be a highly effective force in your treatment.

Jordan's own attitude was exemplary. As he battled cancer, he maintained a meaningful, active lifestyle. He was a consultant to Nike and a trustee of the Lance Armstrong Foundation. He was a board member of privately held Proxima Therapeutics, as well as two nonprofit organizations: the Multiple Myeloma Research Foundation and the Lasker Foundation.

He and his wife, a pediatric oncology nurse, also founded one of the nation's first nonprofit camps for children with cancer—Camp Sunshine in Decatur, Georgia.

In an interview, Jordan said, "It's very powerful for a child who is newly diagnosed with cancer to go to Camp Sunshine, to have a friend or counselor who has the same cancer they had, who has been cured or had a limb amputated, or is bald. It has a powerful effect on the attitudes of these children."

Today Camp Sunshine offers a year-round program, including 24-hour onsite medical and psychological support. It currently serves more than 500 kids and is free of charge to all families.

Hamilton said he would always remember his "raw fear" at his initial diagnosis. But he also said he would never forget the focus, realization, and sense of purpose his cancer brought him, too. He called it "the ironic blessing."

In his book, Jordan writes, "A life-threatening disease like cancer casts our life and purpose in sharp relief. Some cancer patients allow cancer to dominate and define their lives. . . . But there are many, many more who use their illness to find new meaning in their lives. And these are the patients who greatly exceed their prognosis or medical expectation."

Jordan did. He lived 22 years beyond his initial cancer diagnosis, finally succumbing to the disease at 63.

How can we honor his memory? Sending a donation to Camp Sunshine is one possibility. Trying to emulate the courage and compassion he showed in life is another. At the very least, we can all acknowledge a simple truth:

There really is no such thing as a bad day.   ■

THE ANTIDOTE
FOR GREED

At a conference in Las Vegas last July, I participated in a panel discussion called "Libertarian Millionaires: How to Make It, How to Spend It, How to Give It Away."

I write about making it and spending it all the time. Here are a few thoughts on giving it away.

The English architect John Foster once remarked that the loudest laugh in hell is reserved for the man who dies rich. (Presumably because the decedent had neither the enjoyment of spending it nor the pleasure of giving it away.)

We've all heard that shrouds don't have pockets and hearses don't have luggage racks. But that doesn't mean giving your money away isn't a challenge.

Most of us struggle to earn a decent amount, spend a reasonable amount, and save and invest as much as we can. Unless we plan, charitable giving can get short shrift.

However, we want to give in a way that's practical and meaningful. So we grapple with who should get it, when we should give it, and how much we should give.

These are deeply personal questions, of course. And I'm no more certain of the answers than the next guy. Fortunately, we have a few millennia of wise commentary to guide us.

According to the medieval philosopher Moses Maimonides, for instance, there are eight grades of charity:

1. To give reluctantly
2. To give cheerfully, but not adequately
3. To give cheerfully and adequately, but only after being asked
4. To give cheerfully, adequately, and of your own free will, but to put it in the recipient's hand in such a way as to make him feel lesser
5. To let the recipient know who the donor is, but not the reverse
6. To know who is receiving your charity but to remain anonymous to him
7. To have neither the donor nor the recipient be aware of the other's identity
8. To dispense with charity altogether, by enabling your fellow humans to have the wherewithal to earn their own living

This ladder provides a good gauge of our charitable disposition. If we want to move up, we need only ask how to get started and when.

The answer to the second question is easy. Now. It's a mistake—albeit a comforting one—to imagine we'll start giving when we reach a certain income level or net worth.

Like studying or exercising, giving only becomes ingrained when we engage in it regularly. If you aren't charitably disposed now, becoming rich isn't likely to make you so. That makes it imperative to give along the way.

Many of us already are. According to the Giving USA Foundation, the leading researcher on philanthropy, two-thirds of U.S. households with incomes of less than $100,000 give to charity.

Americans gave away over $300 billion in 2007, the most recent year that figures are available. That makes the U.S. the most charitable nation in the world. And not just in terms of the gross amount given . . .

According to a recent study by the Charitable Aid Foundation, Americans give twice as much (1.67 percent of GDP) as the next most charitable nation, the U.K. In fact, Americans give more as a percent of GDP than France, Germany, Turkey, Singapore, New Zealand, and the Netherlands combined.

How much should you give personally? Some say 3 percent of after-tax income is a good goal. Tithers strive for 10 percent. The well-to-do often give much more. Ultimately, *you* must decide.

Mary Hunt, the creator and editor of the website Debt-Proof Living (www.cheapskatemonthly.com), says her family continued to give 10 percent of their after-tax income to charity even while digging out from more than $100,000 in credit card and other unsecured debt.

Some financial planners would argue that it's foolish to contribute to charity while paying exorbitant interest rates. Hunt disagrees. She says she could have paid the debt down faster—it took 13 years—but is convinced the donations helped provide the discipline to make her debt free.

She believes in regular, systematic giving, calling it "the antidote for greed."

There are other benefits of charitable giving. Yes, you'll receive a tax deduction. True, it may force you to better manage the rest of your money. And, if your giving is sizable, you may receive public recognition.

All good. But you'll also feel better about yourself and appreciate more the blessings in your own life.

This doesn't require money, incidentally. As Maimonides reminds us in level eight, we can do more than just share our riches with another. We can reveal to him his own.

Time spent helping others do more for themselves can be the highest form of giving. Give a man a fish and he'll eat for a day. Teach a man to fish . . . and he'll sit in a boat and drink beer all day. (Sorry, but you already knew the original chestnut.)

Money, of course, is the way most organizations get things done. But dollars and cents are only one kind of gift.

Those of lesser means can always give a portion of themselves, whether through a thoughtful act, a timely suggestion, a helpful idea, or a word of appreciation.

As John D. Rockefeller Jr. observed, "Giving is the secret of a healthy life. Not necessarily money, but whatever a man has of encouragement, sympathy and understanding."

In the end, our worth is determined by the good works we *do*, not the fine emotions we *feel*.

And while we may not always have happiness, it is always possible to give it.   ∎

THE GREATEST VIRTUE . . . AND THE FIRST

Frustrated with your job? Bored at home? Would you like your days to be filled with excitement, adventure and a strong sense of purpose?

If so, you can volunteer to work alongside my nephew Conrad Schwalbe. Conrad is a U.S. Marine in Iraq. Currently, he spends his days searching for weapons and clearing houses in Ramadi.

Aside from never knowing whether the house he's about to walk into is booby-trapped—he's already lost several members of his company—there are other inconveniences. Like improvised explosive devices. And snipers.

Then there are the minor inconveniences: missing several meals in a row, staying up for more than a day at a time, going a week or more without a shower, getting woken at night by mortars and gunfire.

My intention is not to drag anyone into an argument about the occupation in Iraq. This message is about gratitude. More than 2,000 years ago, Cicero called it "not only the greatest of virtues, but the parent of all others."

Psychologists say it's virtually impossible to feel grateful and unhappy at the same time.

Gratitude is usually generated in one of two ways. One, by feeling a genuine appreciation for the life that you were given and, two, by making a conscious decision to practice looking at what's right in your life rather than focusing on what's missing.

I'm thankful I don't spend my days knocking on doors in Ramadi, for example. Beyond the U.S. mission in Iraq, I'm grateful for all the men and women in uniform who are willing to lay down their lives for us. George Orwell was right when he said we sleep peaceably in our beds at night only because rough men stand ready to do violence on our behalf.

Of course, if you have nothing more than good health and the love and affection of your family, you have much to be grateful for. But take a moment, too, to marvel at how fortunate you are just to have been born in the modern era.

Your ancestors four generations removed would marvel at contemporary life: Unlimited food at affordable prices . . . plagues that killed millions—polio, smallpox, measles, rickets—all but eradicated . . . the end of backbreaking physical toil for most wage earners . . . the advent of instantaneous global communication and same-day travel to distant cities . . . mass home ownership with central heat and air and limitless modern conveniences . . . senior citizens cared for financially and medically, ending the fear of impoverished old age.

Nor should we forget how advances in medical technology and nutrition have created the greatest human accomplishment of all time—the near doubling of the average lifespan over the last hundred years. (At the beginning of the twentieth century, the average American lived just 41 years.)

Please don't kid yourself that things were really better in "the good old days." As I once heard an historian remark, "If you really believe life was better a hundred years ago, I have just one word for you—dentistry."

Let's appreciate, too, the many political freedoms—denied to millions around the world—that we enjoy today: freedom of expression, freedom of assembly, freedom of religion, and freedom from conscription, among others.

Sure, the federal government has become too big, too intrusive, and too coercive. But let's put things in perspective. Even David

Boaz of the libertarian Cato Institute writes that "Americans today are more free than any people in history. We should take a moment to reflect on our history, and celebrate what we've achieved after centuries of hard work and political struggle."

When you think about it, it's really nothing less than astonishing that you're sitting here reading this at all.

In *A Short History of Nearly Everything,* Bill Bryson writes that "you have been extremely—make that miraculously—fortunate in your personal ancestry. Consider the fact that for 3.8 billion years, a period of time older than the Earth's mountains and rivers and oceans, every one of your forebears on both sides has been attractive enough to find a mate, healthy enough to reproduce, and sufficiently blessed by fate and circumstances to live long enough to do so. Not one of your pertinent ancestors was squashed, devoured, drowned, starved, stranded, stuck fast, untimely wounded, or otherwise deflected from its life's quest of delivering a tiny charge of genetic material to the right partner at the right moment in order to perpetuate the only possible sequence of hereditary combinations that could result—eventually, astoundingly, and all too briefly—in you."

Meditate on that for a moment. And recognize that the odds against you being here are astronomically large. Then be grateful . . .

Gratitude makes you feel like you have enough. Ingratitude leaves us in a state of deprivation where we are always looking for something else.

Don't just feel grateful, however. Do something about it. As William Arthur Ward once said, "Feeling gratitude and not expressing it is like wrapping a present and not giving it."

Let your coworkers know, in subtle ways, that you enjoy working with them. Show your friends that you don't take their companionship for granted. Let your partner know how you really feel.

Who knows? You may be surprised to learn how they feel about you. Doing this is a good thing, by the way. Medical studies consistently show that people who express gratitude regularly are happier, healthier, and less susceptible to depression.

So find a moment to appreciate your incredible good fortune . . . and let the people around you know how you feel.

As the Chinese philosopher Lao Tzu wrote more than 2,000 years ago:

If you look to others for fulfillment,
you will never truly be fulfilled.
If your happiness depends on money,
you will never be happy with yourself.
Be content with what you have;
rejoice in the way things are.
When you realize there is nothing lacking,
the whole world belongs to you.

■ WHO'S YOUR CITY?

We all make at least three important decisions in our lives: what to do, where to do it, and with whom.

We devote a lot of time to choosing our livelihood and nurturing our careers. We try, too, to choose the right life partner—someone who offers us unconditional love and support.

But the third factor also has a powerful impact on our financial prospects, life experiences, and general level of happiness: *where we live*. Polls show that where we live is more important to our happiness than education or even how much we earn.

According to the U.S. Census Bureau, the average American moves once every seven years. More than 40 million people relocate each year; 15 million of them move more than 50 miles.

Some move for job opportunities, others to get closer to family. Still others are upsizing or downsizing, leaving the frostbelt for the sunbelt, or simply getting out of the rat race while they can still run.

Where we live is the precursor to almost everything we do. As Richard Florida writes in *Who's Your City?*:

> The place we choose to live affects every aspect of our being. It can determine the income we earn, the people we meet, the friends we make, the partners we choose, and the options available to our children and families. People are not equally happy everywhere, and some places do a better job of providing a high quality of life than others. Some places offer us more vibrant labor

markets, better career prospects, higher real estate appreciation, and stronger investment and earning opportunities. Some places offer more promising mating markets. Others are better environments for raising children.

Location can also provide a hedge against some of life's unpleasant surprises. Jobs often end. Relationships can, too.

As Florida writes, "It's exponentially easier to get back on your feet when your location has a vibrant economy with lots of jobs to choose from, or a lot of eligible single people in your age range to date."

Of course, millions remain rooted right where they were born. The climate may be too cold, the economic opportunities limited, or the singles market nonexistent. Yet they stay. Why? Some lack the economic resources. Others are frightened by change or uncertainty.

But many—perhaps most—stay put for the best of reasons. They love their hometown. Their biggest priority is spending their lives with lifelong friends and family. Often they have chosen community over economic opportunity—or other potential advantages—and found it a worthwhile trade-off.

The rise of technology and economic prosperity, however, are giving more of us the freedom to relocate.

As a writer, for example, my office is wherever I plop down with my laptop. (A big change from all those years on Wall Street when I was chained to my desk.) I am free to live virtually anywhere. But "anywhere" can be a bit daunting.

Do you choose a stunning natural environment or the excitement of city life? Do you go with a warm year-round climate or a lovely change of seasons? Do you enjoy all the amenities of the big city or the easy familiarity and laidback lifestyle of a small or mid-sized town?

My answer is "all of the above." I'd be happy just to rotate.

Unfortunately, that suggestion provoked a minor insurrection from my wife and daughter, both decided nesters. Plus, the kids are in school nine months a year. (Guess I'm not Jonathan Livingston Seagull after all.)

Today there are plenty of places around the country that offer good schools, affordable housing, high quality health care, and economic opportunity. But with the freedom to go *anywhere,* some are searching for even more.

They are looking for a place that makes them feel energized. A place that offers great aesthetics, as well as cultural and recreational opportunities. A place that provides a sense of pride and attachment.

Most of us, in fact, have already found it. Gallup reports that 67 percent of Americans are happy with where they live, rating their community satisfaction a 4 or 5 on a five-point scale.

But that still leaves nearly a third who are either ambivalent or dissatisfied with where they live. If you're part of this group, you may know exactly where you'd rather be. But if you're not sure, you might benefit from Florida's book.

He offers a smorgasbord of factors to consider when choosing a new location. He also suggests the best cities for singles, for recent college graduates, for young couples, mid-career professionals, families with children, empty nesters, and retirees. Some of us his choices are surprising. All of them are well researched, taking in everything from educational, cultural, and recreational opportunities to the local job market, taxes, and the cost of living.

If you want more personalized advice, visit Bert Sperling's free website: www.bestplaces.net/fybp/. It allows you to customize your search based on the job market, climate, health care, education, recreation, arts and culture, and other criteria. His goal? To help you "Find Your Best Place."

Of course, you may wonder what the people will be like when you get there. Here's a hint:

Author Wayne Dyer once said he was walking along the beach in his hometown and bumped into a couple who had just moved there.

"What are the people like here?" the woman asked. "We're curious."

"What were they like where you came from?" asked Dyer.

The woman frowned. "Not too nice, really," she said. "Most of them were cold and unfriendly. No one ever really reached out."

Dyer nodded his head. "I think you'll find they're that way *here*, too."

A few months later, he ran into another couple who had just moved to town. They too inquired what the local townspeople were like.

"What were they like where you came from?" asked Dyer.

"Oh, they were great," the woman gushed. "Everybody was so sweet and friendly. They were like family."

Dyer nodded his head: "I think you'll find they're that way *here*, too." ∎

THE HEALING OF
KAREN ARMSTRONG

Nineteenth-century philosopher Arthur Schopenhauer was one of history's great pessimists.

His view of life was unremittingly dark. Yet even the old crepe-hanger himself believed that we are ultimately redeemed by our empathy for our fellow man.

In his essay "On the Foundations of Morality," published in 1839, Schopenhauer wrote, "How is it possible that suffering that is neither my own nor of my concern should immediately affect me as though it were my own, and with such force that it moves me to action? . . . This is something really mysterious, something for which Reason can provide no explanation, and for which no basis can be found in practical experience. It is not unknown even to the most hard-hearted and self-interested. Examples appear every day before our eyes of instant responses in kind, without reflection, one person helping another, coming to his aid, even setting his own life in clear danger for someone whom he has seen for the first time, having nothing more in mind than that the other is in need and peril in his life."

I'm still trying to square these words—which strike most of us as instinctively true—with what happened to Angel Arce Torres in Hartford, Conn., recently.

As the Associated Press reported, "A 78-year-old man is tossed like a rag doll by a hit-and-run driver and lies motionless on a busy street as car after car goes by. Pedestrians gawk but do nothing. One driver stops but then pulls back into traffic. A man on a scooter circles the victim before zipping away. The chilling scene, captured on video by a streetlight surveillance camera—has touched off a round of soul-searching in Hartford, with the capital city's biggest newspaper blaring 'SO INHUMANE' on the front page and the police chief lamenting: 'We no longer have a moral compass.'"

Although it was initially reported that onlookers didn't even bother to call for help, it was later discovered that four people did dial 911 shortly after the accident.

Still, Torres—who is now paralyzed from the neck down—was not only left for dead by the perpetrator, but left unattended by dozens of passers-by.

In the days that followed, hundreds in the national media expressed outrage. It's not my intention here to pile on. Nor do I blame Hartford. If this could happen in one city, it could happen in another, perhaps many others.

However, I would like to make a simple observation. Without compassion, there really isn't much to separate us from the rest of the animal kingdom.

If we're deaf and blind to the suffering of those around us, what is the value of language, intelligence, culture, or technology? Without compassion, what is left to redeem us?

Genuine compassion is not about thinking compassionate thoughts. It's about taking action.

Not just in times of crisis—or during a tragedy like the one in Hartford recently—but every day. After all, there is plenty of suffering in the world right now. We have only to act.

If you haven't seen it, I strongly suggest that you take a few minutes to watch scholar Karen Armstrong's acceptance speech after receiving the TED prize in February. (The annual TED conference is where some of the world's most fascinating thinkers and doers are challenged to give the talk of their lives—in 18 minutes or less.)

In her talk, Armstrong argues that religion is not about believing certain things. "Religion," she says, "is about behaving differently. . . . And religious doctrines are meant to be summons to action: you only understand them when you put them into practice."

I think this is true. You don't have to hold the "right" religious viewpoint—or any religious viewpoint—to be compassionate. You need only be a person of conscience—who acts.

So believe what you will. But recognize that we all have a choice. We can be compassionate . . . or we can be a paler version of the bystanders in Hartford.

The choice is ours. ∎

The Cheapest Medicine . . . and the Best

When I was 11, my friend Rocky Wagner came over for a sleepover.

You really can't really get into too much trouble when you're 11. (That comes later.) But we did our best anyway. We raided the kitchen. We snuck out the window. We got into my parents' Cold Duck. (Not bad.)

Around 2 A.M., however, my Mom startled me when she flicked on the hallway light just as we were creeping in the front door, and I spilled a bucket of tadpoles in the foyer.

Exactly why I was carrying a bucket of tadpoles around at two in the morning eludes me now. But I vividly recall a couple hundred of them wriggling around on the floor—and that my mother was not amused.

At least, she wasn't *then*. Now, apparently, it was *hilarious*. She practically tears up every time she tells this story. And she remembers every detail. ("They were pollywogs, not tadpoles.")

Funny how time changes our perceptions.

My friend Rodney, for example, has a foot that is badly scarred. When he was walking to school in first grade, a woman driving by ran over it. Aware that she had hit something, she backed up to get a better look and ran over it *again*. She then got out of the car, set Rodney on the side of the road, and sped off.

You hear this story and want to be appalled. But you can't. Because the way Rodney tells it—with his hangdog expression and deadpan delivery—you end up busting a gut instead.

If we only knew how we'd look back on our troubles someday, maybe we could laugh at them now.

As the British poet Samuel Butler said, "a sense of humor keen enough to show a man his own absurdities, as well as those of other people, will keep him from the commission of all sins, or nearly all, save those that are worth committing."

Science is proving that laughter really is the best medicine. A recent study done at the University of Maryland Medical Center shows a good laugh can lower your blood pressure, protect your heart, improve brain functioning, elevate your mood, and reduce stress.

Laughter is a workout for your diaphragm, as well as your respiratory and facial muscles. It tones intestinal functioning and strengthens the muscles that hold the abdominal organs in place. (Who couldn't use that?)

Hearty laughter can even burn calories equivalent to several minutes on the rowing machine or exercise bike.

And the alternative? As Henry Ward Beecher said, "A person without a sense of humor is like a wagon without springs—jolted by every pebble in the road."

Moreover, studies show that distressing emotions—anger, anxiety, stress, depression—are often related to heart disease. The quickest relief—cheap, effective, and readily available—is a good laugh.

Laughter relaxes us, connects us to others, and enhances our ability to fight disease.

So lighten up. Yes, the economy is bad. You may have more than your fair share of personal problems, too. But as George Bernard Shaw pointed out, "The world does not cease to be funny when people die any more than it ceases to be serious when people laugh."

If the folks in your household aren't exactly filled with mirth right now, try renting an antic movie like *Arthur, Airplane!* or *Young Frankenstein*. (Sorry, my humor isn't terribly highbrow.)

If you're a reader, let me recommend *The Life and Times of the Thunderbolt Kid* by Bill Bryson, *Me Talk Pretty One Day* by David Sedaris, or *Carry On, Jeeves* by the master himself, P.G. Wodehouse— all guaranteed to elicit great gales of laughter.

Stand-up comics can also provide welcome relief when life starts feeling like one damned thing after another.

You can check out a local comedy club or catch a great comic on video. Some of my favorites are Rita Rudner ("My grandmother buried three husbands—and two of them were just napping"), Steven Wright ("I spilled spot remover on my dog. Now he's gone"), Garry Shandling ("They say oysters improve your sex life, but it hasn't worked for me. Maybe I'm putting them on too soon"), and Jeff Foxworthy ("Changing a diaper is kinda like opening a birthday present from your grandmother. You never know what's inside but you're pretty sure you're not gonna like it").

Humor is powerful emotional medicine. It lowers stress, dissolves anger, and unites families. More importantly, it reminds us that our troubles may not be as earthshaking as they appear.

As the Zen monk Shunryu Suzuki said, "When you can laugh at yourself, *there* is enlightenment." ∎

THE SCIENCE OF GIVING

A few months ago, I received a phone call from George Rupp.

Rupp is the President and Chief Executive Officer of the International Rescue Committee (IRC). Founded by Albert Einstein, the IRC serves refugees and communities victimized by oppression or violent conflict. When thousands run from natural disasters, war or repression, the IRC is there, providing food and water, shelter, health care, and education.

Each Thanksgiving for the past few years, I've sent my readers a letter reminding them how incredibly rich our lives are and asking them to remember the IRC, the world's recognized leader in humanitarian emergencies.

I had never heard of George Rupp, however. "I'm just calling to let you how much you've inspired us—our whole organization—with your letter," he said.

Embarrassed, I mumbled something in response.

"We're planning to read it to Tom Brokaw and the other directors at the annual board meeting Wednesday. We'd also like to turn it into a national fundraising letter. Would that be all right with you?"

All right? I felt like I'd just been injected with 100 mL of pure dopamine. I love the IRC. I love sharing its mission.

By the time I got off the phone, my wife said I was acting so goofy I might as well take the rest of the day off. When I walked outside the sky was bluer, the neighbor's dog was friendlier, and the birds, I'm sure, were singing in counterpoint. It was a weird feeling.

But not unusual, perhaps. New studies show that we're actually hardwired to feel good—and live longer—by helping others.

Dr. Stephen Post, a professor of bioethics at Case Western Reserve University's School of Medicine, says, "The remarkably good news is that, over the past ten years, we have about five hundred serious scientific studies that demonstrate the power of [generosity] to enhance health."

You've always known that giving is its own reward. But science has discovered a slew of side benefits.

Here are just a few recent findings:

- Those who start giving in high school usually experience better physical and mental health over the next fifty years.
- Giving reduces mortality later in life too. People who volunteer for two or more organizations have a 44 percent lower likelihood of dying—and that's after sifting out other significant factors like age, gender, marital status, frequency of exercise, smoking habits, etc.
- Giving generates a sense of inner freedom, serenity, and peace that affects the quality of life.
- Giving reduces adolescent depression and suicide risk.
- Giving helps us forgive ourselves, promoting a sense of well-being and greater self-esteem.
- Giving reduces negative emotions, like spite, rage, and envy, that contribute to stress-induced psychological and physical ailments.
- Columbia University psychologist Eva Midlarksy has found that through giving we gain a greater sense of meaning in our lives, cope better with our own stress by shifting our focus to others, feel more socially connected, enjoy a greater sense of competence and effectiveness, and are more likely to live an active lifestyle.

Not bad. And there are many ways to give. Money, of course, is how most organizations get things done. But there are effective ways to donate your time, as well:

- Volunteer. According to Doug Oman of the University of California at Berkeley, "Volunteering is associated with substantial reductions in mortality."
- Create a network of giving. Find others who are isolated or ignored and invite them to join you. Studies show that both of you are likely to benefit.
- Become a mentor. Nothing is more beneficial to the young than connecting with a caring adult who inspires them.
- Pass the torch. Older adults have accumulated a lifetime of wisdom and experience. Recognize your own value—and share it with others.

Biologist David Sloan Wilson says, "We have said since millennia—in fact, this has been a fundamental tenet of religion—that if you do good things, it will reflect back to you, not immediately, not every time, but in general. This is a deeply entrenched notion."

Now science is confirming it.

Giving is a simple act. Yet studies show that generous behavior may do more to protect and extend your health than vitamin supplements, green tea, fish oil, or an aspirin a day.

Each of us is flawed in a hundred ways. But giving redeems us. It ennobles us. It helps us create a better version of ourselves.

In his book *Why Good Things Happen to Good People,* Dr. Post writes, "You wish to be happy? Loved? Safe? Secure? You want to turn to others in tough times and count on them? You want the warmth of true connection? You'd like to walk into the world each day knowing that this is a place of benevolence and hope? Then I have one answer: give. Give daily, in small ways, and you will be happier. Give, and you will be healthier. Give, and you will even live longer."

There are many worthy organizations that would welcome your time and money. To learn more about the fabulous work of the International Rescue Committee, feel free to visit theirc.org. ■

ARE YOU KEEPING THE EMBERS ALIVE?

Back in 1999, when the Internet bubble was in full swing, my employer, an investment firm, announced plans to open the world's first Internet-based global trading website.

Investors would have the ability to buy online virtually any stock, traded on any exchange in the world, 24 hours a day. On this exciting news, our stock—which had been trading in the basement—shot up more than tenfold.

That was both good and bad. Good, because in the company pension plan I owned more shares than anyone outside the executive suite. Bad, because the company chairman, who was also a good friend, wouldn't allow me to sell them.

This bothered me, to put it mildly. Especially since I knew there was no chance that website was ever going to fly.

Making a market in a foreign stock when the local market is closed is a risky business under the best of circumstances. To even offer a valid quote, a market maker generally has to have a dialogue with the trader to find out whether he is a buyer or seller, how many shares he wants to move, and so on.

This isn't what most people imagine when they envision making an online trade.

In addition, foreign companies often make major announcements, in dozens of different languages, after their markets close. Offering shares to investors—or buying theirs—before knowing the local market's reaction to that news can send you to the poor-house quick.

Moreover, our firm had so far done no more than hire a web-master. We didn't have a functioning website yet. We didn't have online clients. The wild run-up in our stock—like so many others at the time—was based on the sheerest speculation.

It confirmed my view that the investor mania for all things Internet-related was nothing more than hysteria and wishful thinking. Technology traders had simply come unhinged. And I really, **really** wanted to unload my shares while buyers were in such an optimistic mood.

But my friend, the company chairman, adamantly refused. "The only way you can sell those shares," he chided me, an employee of 14 years, "is if you leave the company."

So I left.

That didn't improve matters. My firm sued me, dragged its feet, and still wouldn't distribute my pension shares. My attorney threat-ened legal action for breach of fiduciary duties.

After several months, I finally got my shares. By then, the world's first global trading website was a publicly acknowledged flop. And the stock—surprise, surprise—had plummeted, coming to rest at a dollar a share.

To say this ate at me would be an understatement. My shares were worth over a million dollars less. I was angry about the lost opportunity. Angry, especially, at my former friend and colleague.

Someone once said it's easier to forgive your enemies than your friends. I think that's true. (After all, you don't expect much from your enemies.) Still, it's better to forgive them both.

In my experience, keeping old scores makes you less than what you are. It makes you bitter, keeps you nettled. It creates a burden you don't need to carry.

Occasionally, I'll hear an irate friend or neighbor say "I'll for-give him. But I'll never forget." But what's the point? That's just another way of saying you're still packing your resentments around with you.

"But the S.O.B. doesn't deserve to be forgiven," a woman once said of her ex-husband. Perhaps not. But it does no good to dwell on it. Why keep the embers alive?

As William H. Walton said "To carry a grudge is like being stung to death by one bee."

For my part, I let go of my anger toward my friend years ago. Today it just seems like "one of those things," a misunderstanding that ballooned into something more a long time ago.

Frankly, I wish I'd been wise enough to reach that mindset a lot sooner. After all, none of us can change the past. And you aren't really free until you've put your grievances behind you.

If you still find yourself feeling resentful about something that happened long ago, do yourself a favor. Let it go.

You may believe that some behavior is simply inexcusable. And in certain cases, it is. But even then, you don't have to forgive someone for his sake. Do it for your own.

As Confucius told us 2,500 years ago: To be wronged is nothing unless you continue to remember it.

PART FOUR

THE SEARCH FOR MEANING

Of the thousands of questions I've received from *Spiritual Wealth* readers, the toughest may be "Could you explain, briefly, what you mean when you use the word *spiritual?*"

Probably not.

Talking about spirituality is easy. Defining it in just a few words is more difficult. (Even an abridged dictionary can yield more than a dozen definitions.)

Our inability to nail down this word reminds me of Justice Potter Stewart's famous declaration. We may not be able to define spirituality but "we know it when we see it."

And when we see it, we like to put a one-word label on it: believer, Christian, Jew, Muslim, agnostic, skeptic, atheist, whatever.

When I write about spiritual issues, readers often implore me to tell them "what I believe."

What I believe, of course, is the subject of every essay in this book. Yet this is too ambiguous—and ultimately unsatisfactory—to many. They want a declaration, a single word that encapsulates what I believe.

Yet that is not always possible . . . or even desirable.

Concert pianist Vladimir Horowitz once played a dissonant composition at a private gathering. When he finished, a guest asked,

"I don't understand what that composition means, Mr. Horowitz. Could you please explain it?" Without a word, Horowitz played the piece again. When he finished, he turned to his questioner and said, "That's what it means."

For some people, a one-word description of their spiritual beliefs is both easy and accurate. More often than not, however, the question is asked for the purpose of making a snap judgment. It's a short cut to "I already agree with you" or "I don't agree with you, therefore I won't listen to you."

Some seekers have tried to explain their nontraditional beliefs with clever phraseology. Religion scholar Karen Armstrong describes herself as a "freelance monotheist." Albert Einstein called himself a "deeply religious nonbeliever."

But those who bother to inquire generally want specificity. And readers—including pastors who have asked permission to use my work—often ask what religious view I'm trying to promote.

I'm not trying to promote any particular line of religious thinking. Nor am I trying to promote nonreligious thinking. My goal is much more modest. I'm just trying to promote *thinking*.

Judging by some of my emails, that's not always easy. But I'm fine with anyone who disagrees with my views or hits the "Unsubscribe" button. I don't have an agenda. And there is plenty to choose from out there in the *spiritual marketplace*, from the severest fundamentalism to "the healing power of crystals."

However, it may be that many readers have stuck with me on this sensitive topic precisely because I know I don't have all the answers. Moreover, I'm skeptical of anyone who claims he or she does.

There's a lot of wisdom in the old saying, "Trust those who seek the truth; doubt those who find it."

Humility is cherished in every religious tradition. Yet how can we be humble if we hold our beliefs with pride or arrogance? Doubt is an essential component of humility. We should all allow for the possibility that our beliefs—especially about the ineffable— could be mistaken.

Reverend Alan Jones, Dean of Grace Cathedral, once observed that, "The opposite of faith is not doubt. The opposite of faith is certainty."

Similarly, in *A New Earth*, Eckhart Tolle writes, "Having a belief system—a set of thoughts that you regard as the absolute truth—does not make you spiritual no matter what the nature of those beliefs is. In fact, the more you make your thoughts (beliefs) into your identity, the more cut off you are from the spiritual dimension within yourself."

My own religious background is fairly traditional. I grew up attending Trinity Episcopal church in Staunton, Virginia, where I was taught the stories of the Bible and the morality of the New Testament. In our household, we said a blessing before meals and our prayers at night.

As a passionate reader, however, I also learned a bit about other world religions and the earth's natural history. Over time I began to question some of the things I learned in church.

Many readers, I'm sure, have had a similar experience. We all recognize—or should—that the religious traditions we're taught as children are highly dependent on where and when we were born and what our parents believed.

Most would also agree that the best scientific thinking cannot be found in a 2,000-year-old text.

Yet there are core spiritual principles common to all religions as well as compassionate secular philosophies. We can focus on sectarian differences or we can emphasize the points of agreement that unite us.

In *Spiritual Wealth*, I took the latter path. What follows are a few of my thoughts on life's biggest questions—and the search for meaning in a material world.

DISCOVERING THE LAWS
OF LIFE

In 1985, I began working with an international money management firm in Winter Park, Florida.

Although I was young and wet behind the ears, I soon discovered I had "the Midas touch." When it came to investing, everything I touched turned into a muffler.

I fooled around with options and futures. Got burned with micro-caps and junior gold-mining companies. Tried all sorts of dubious trading strategies with equally dubious results.

My more-experienced colleagues had plenty of investment opinions they were eager to share with me. Most, I learned, were worth about what I paid for them.

Things might never have turned around for me had I not become a devotee of investment legend John Templeton.

Templeton died last year at the age of 95. Today the world is a lesser place. Few American success stories can rival this one . . .

Templeton was born in Winchester, Tennessee, in 1912 and was the first from his small farming town to attend college: Yale University.

However, with his family squeezed by the Depression, it appeared his tuition and board could not be paid. Yet, always a little sharper than his contemporaries, Templeton made up the shortfall with his dormitory poker winnings.

He graduated from Yale in 1934, winning a Rhodes scholarship to Oxford University where he received a masters degree in law.

When war broke out in Europe in 1939, the stock market tanked. Templeton borrowed $10,000 and bought 100 shares each in 104 companies whose shares were trading at $1 or less. Four of them became worthless. He locked in dramatic gains in the others.

The following year he bought a small investment firm that became the foundation of his investment empire. In the years that followed, he launched and managed some of the world's largest and most successful international mutual funds. Almost single-handedly, he pioneered the art of global investing, avidly seeking out the world's most promising investment opportunities wherever they resided.

In the 1950s, for example, he poured shareholders' money into the Tokyo stock market, buying then-obscure companies like Hitachi and Fuji. With the wounds of WWII still fresh, investing in Japan was about as popular with Americans then as the idea of funding the Taliban today. But as Japan's battered economy was rebuilt, he earned outsized returns for his investors.

This is rarer than you might imagine. Each year, more than three-quarters of all equity fund managers fail to beat the market. Templeton did it regularly—and he did it for decades.

$10,000 invested in the S&P 500 54 years ago, with dividends reinvested, would have turned into more than $2 million. Not bad. But the same amount invested in his flagship Templeton Growth Fund would have grown to $9 million.

During his long career, Templeton earned a reputation as one of the world's undisputed money masters. *Forbes* magazine once described him as "one of the handful of true investment greats in a field crowded with mediocrity and bloated reputations."

He sold his Templeton funds to the Franklin Group for $440 million in 1992. But he remained an active investor well into his nineties.

At the height of the Internet bubble, for instance, Templeton sold short dozens of young technology companies just before their shares came out of "lock-up," the six-month cooling off period following an IPO. He made over $80 million in a matter of weeks. Years later he still referred to it as "the easiest money I ever made."

Templeton knew what it meant to be a true contrarian. "To buy when others are despondently selling and to sell when others are avidly buying requires the greatest fortitude," he said, "and pays the greatest reward."

Over the years, Templeton's money management skills and uncommon sense helped thousands of investors reach their investment goals. In the process, he became one of the world's wealthiest men himself.

However, his investment acumen was only one reason I admired him. Another was his philosophy of life.

Templeton was a great believer that true wealth doesn't come from accumulating money or things, but from fulfilling a purpose outside ourselves, whether that's exercising our talents, raising our kids to be happy, productive adults, or contributing to our communities in some meaningful way.

As Templeton was fond of saying, "Happiness pursued eludes, happiness given returns."

He wrote or edited ten books on spiritual development. He endowed a business and management school, Templeton College, at Oxford. In 1987, Queen Elizabeth II knighted him for his philanthropy.

Twenty-one years ago, he established The John Templeton Foundation—with a current endowment of $1.5 billion—and created the world's richest annual award, the $1.6 million Templeton Prize for new discoveries in the realm of the human spirit.

For Templeton, it was not enough to dominate the worlds of investing and philanthropy. He wanted to make an impact on the world of ideas. And his overriding goal was to reconcile the diverse and often conflicting worlds of science, philosophy, and religion.

Today the Templeton Foundation gives out more than $70 million annually for academic research in such diverse fields as theoretical physics, cosmology, evolutionary biology, and cognitive science.

"No human has yet grasped 1% of what can be known about spiritual realities," insisted Templeton. His foundation exists to promote character development, ethical living, and greater spiritual understanding.

As he told *BusinessWeek* in 2005, "I grew up Presbyterian. Presbyterians thought the Methodists were wrong. Catholics thought all Protestants were wrong. The Jews thought the Christians were wrong. So, what I'm financing is humility. I want people to realize that you shouldn't think you know it all."

In his 1994 book *Discovering the Laws of Life,* Templeton argued that the laws of human behavior operate nearly as predictability as the laws of science. The exercise of truthfulness, reliability, perseverance, forgiveness, gratitude, tolerance, reverence, humility, and compassion will almost certainly attract good things in your life, just as surely as their opposites bring trouble and misery.

Templeton wanted us to know this. He made it his mission. "I'm only going to be on this planet once, and for a short time," he said. "What can I do with my life that will lead to permanent benefits?"

Templeton knew a great deal about how to make money, how to invest it, and how to give it away. But he also understood deeper realities.

In his book *The Templeton Plan,* he quotes 19th century abolitionist and social reformer Henry Ward Beecher:

"No man can tell whether he is rich or poor by turning to his ledger. It is the heart that makes a man rich. He is rich according to what he is, not according to what he has."

Sadly, John Templeton is dead. Long live John Templeton. ■

THE SAGE OF
MONTICELLO

I recently visited Monticello again, home of one of my all-time favorite Americans, Thomas Jefferson.

Jefferson, of course, is best known as a Founding Father. He was the principal author of The Declaration of Independence, laying down the foundations of self-government and individual freedoms. (The preamble established, for the first time in history, the concept of human rights as the basis for a republic.)

Jefferson served as delegate to the Virginia General Assembly and to Congress, as governor of Virginia, minister to France, secretary of state, vice president, and president from 1801 to 1809.

As President of the United States, he sponsored the Lewis and Clark expedition and doubled the size of the country with the Louisiana Purchase.

He later founded the University of Virginia in Charlottesville.

A child of the Enlightenment, he was also one of the country's great Renaissance men.

Jefferson was a statesman, parliamentarian, historian, surveyor, philosopher, scientist, diplomat, architect, inventor, educator, lawyer, farmer, breeder, manufacturer, botanist, horticulturalist, anthropologist, meteorologist, astronomer, paleontologist, lexicologist, linguist, ethnologist, Biblicist, mathematician, geographer, librarian, bibliophile, classicist, scholar, bibliographer, translator, writer, editor, musician, gastronome, and connoisseur of wine.

(It's hard to reflect on Jefferson's life without feeling like a bit of an underachiever.)

When John F. Kennedy welcomed a group of 49 Nobel Prize winners to a dinner in their honor at The White House in 1962, he toasted them saying, "I think this is the most extraordinary collection of talent, of human knowledge, that has ever been gathered together at the White House—with the possible exception of when Thomas Jefferson dined alone."

Jefferson was an avid reader in English, Spanish, French, Greek, and Latin. His personal library contained nearly 10,000 volumes.

"I cannot live without books," he wrote his friend John Adams in 1815.

When the British destroyed the library in Washington during the War of 1812, Jefferson offered his personal collection to start a new one. It became the foundation of the Library of Congress.

Jefferson, of course, was not without his flaws.

His political rival Alexander Hamilton saw Jefferson's politics as "tinctured with fanaticism." John Nicholas, clerk of Jefferson's Albermarle County, told George Washington that Jefferson was "one of the most artful, intriguing, industrious, and double-faced politicians in all America."

And, like most plantation owners of his time, he was a slaveholder.

He was troubled by slavery all his life, calling it "this hideous blot." An early draft of the Declaration—voted down by his compatriots—called for an end to the slave trade.

But whatever his personal feelings, he remained a slaveholder throughout his life. Upon his death, he freed only his mistress Sally Hemmings and her children.

Today Jefferson rests under a magnificent granite monument at the Monticello Graveyard. Sally Hemmings' grave, according to Jefferson biographer Christopher Hitchens, "lies somewhere under the parking lot of the Hampton Inn at Charlottesville."

Jefferson's strong beliefs and contradictory actions, says Hitchens, shows that history is often "a tragedy and not a morality tale."

Jefferson was conflicted about slavery, in part, because he was a serious student of ethics. Posted at Monticello, for example, are his Ten Canons for Practical Life:

1. Never put off to tomorrow what you can do today.
2. Never trouble another for what you can do yourself.
3. Never spend money before you have it.
4. Never buy what you do not want, because it is cheap; it will be dear to you.
5. Pride costs us more than hunger, thirst, and cold.
6. We never repent of having eaten too little.
7. Nothing is troublesome that we do willingly.
8. How much pain have cost us the evils which have never happened.
9. Take things always by their smooth handle.
10. When angry, count ten, before you speak; if very angry, an hundred.

His letters to family and friends were often punctuated with practical or ethical advice.

"Never suppose that in any possible situation or under any circumstances that is best for you to do a dishonorable thing however slightly so it may appear to you," he wrote Peter Carr in 1785. "Whenever you are to do a thing though it can never be known but to yourself, ask yourself how you would act were all the world looking at you, and act accordingly."

Jefferson was also an early advocate of religious tolerance. He was a vigorous proponent of the separation of church and state and authored the Virginia Statute for Religious Freedom.

In his "Notes on the State of Virginia" he wrote, "It does me no injury for my neighbor to say there are twenty gods or no god. It neither picks my pocket nor breaks my leg."

Jefferson counted himself a Unitarian, but he often said he was the member of a sect that included no one but himself.

Jefferson accepted the social teachings of the New Testament but rejected the miracle stories. Working alone in 1800, he took a razor and paste and cobbled together his own version of the "authentic" sayings of Jesus of Nazareth. The result was the Jefferson Bible, still in print today.

Predictably, this act outraged many of his contemporaries.

Assailed by Christian fundamentalists during the election of 1800, Jefferson wrote, "They believe that any portion of power confided to me, will be exerted in opposition to their schemes. And they believe rightly; for I have sworn upon the altar of God, eternal hostility against every form of tyranny over the mind of man."

Jefferson's unwillingness to be bound by any dogma helped create—and codify—the religious pluralism that we enjoy today.

He told Adam Smith that 50 or 60 years of religious reading could be summed up in just four words, "be just and good."

"I never told my own religion, nor scrutinized that of another," he wrote Margaret Bayard Smith in 1816. "It is in our lives, and not from our words, that our religion must be read." ■

THE WOLF IN MONK'S ROBES

In 2008 more than 100 deaths were reported in Tibet, as the Chinese government cracked down on demonstrators in Lhasa demanding greater autonomy.

In many ways, this is nothing new.

In 1950, Chairman Mao Zedong ordered the "liberation" of Tibet. The Chinese army occupied the country and the following year it was turned into a so-called "autonomous region."

Since Tibet is a relatively poor country with no oil and little strategic value, the rest of the world decried the thuggery but essentially did nothing. The Dalai Lama was forced to escape in 1959, and he remains the country's spiritual leader and head of the Tibetan government-in-exile.

Today he concedes that genuine independence is no longer a realistic goal for Tibet. But he supports greater freedom and autonomy for his people.

The Dalai Lama condemned the violence of the protestors, however, and threatened to step down as leader of the movement unless it stopped. "Violence for us is suicide," he said.

Yet because the Nobel Peace Prize winner remains a high-profile symbol of resistance to Chinese oppression, the government there continues to demonize him. At one meeting, for example, Tibet's Communist Party chief said, "The Dalai is a wolf in monk's robes, a devil with a human face but the heart of a beast."

The Dalai Lama does not dispute this assessment. Not because it's accurate, but because he believes angry words like these are "the wind blowing behind your back." And he views the speaker not with disdain, but with compassion.

"For a spiritual practitioner," he says, "one's enemies play a crucial role. . . . Our friends do not ordinarily test us and provide the opportunity to cultivate patience; only our enemies do this. So, from this standpoint we can consider our enemy as a great teacher, and revere them for giving us this precious opportunity."

This is a radical approach to diplomacy—and to personal relationships, as well. He believes those who confront or defy us provide the resistance necessary to build inner strength.

And despite being a high priest, the Dalai Lama doesn't feel we need to adopt his Buddhist beliefs to benefit from this approach. Many Westerners, accustomed to proselytizers, are surprised to hear this.

In his book *Ethics for the New Millennium,* he writes, "Spirituality I take to be concerned with those qualities of the human spirit—such as love and compassion, patience, tolerance, forgiveness, contentment, a sense of responsibility, a sense of harmony—which bring happiness to both self and others . . . My call for a spiritual revolution is thus not a call for religious revolution. Rather, it is a call for a radical reorientation away from our habitual preoccupation with self."

This is not a message you typically hear from world religious leaders. Yet if this viewpoint were widely adopted, imagine how things might look today in the Middle East or between India and Pakistan.

In essence, this "wolf in monk's robes" reminds us that the essence of religion is not our beliefs. Rather, it is about improving ourselves.

"The very purpose of religion is to control yourself, not to criticize others," he writes. "How much am I doing about my anger? About my attachment, about my hatred, about my pride, my jealousy? These are the things which we must check in daily life."

The Dalai Lama is hardly the first spiritual leader to take this point of view.

As the Anglican priest William R. Inge said more than a half century ago, "Religion is a way of walking, not a way of talking." ∎

FROM GRAND TRUTHS TO GRAND CAVERNS

Two summers ago, I toured Grand Caverns in the Shenandoah Valley.

It is an oasis of subterranean beauty. Awestruck, I walked from one room to the next, surrounded by shimmering red and yellow walls, giant stalagmites, and crystal-clear pools from underground streams. Near the end of the tour, I asked our guide—a girl of high-school age who was probably working a summer job—the approximate age of the caverns.

"Less than 6,000 years," she answered.

"6,000 years?" I said, incredulous. "But these caverns must be millions of years old."

"Well, I'm a Pentecostal," she explained. "And since we believe the earth is only 6,000 years old, the caverns *can't* be any older than that."

"What if you were Presbyterian," I asked with a wink. "How old would the caverns be then?"

She gave me a puzzled look and said she didn't understand the question. We left it at that.

I learned later that geologists estimate the caverns were formed more than 400 million years ago during the Paleozoic era. (In case you were wondering.)

Ah, the age-old conflict between science and religion. Of all the religious wars, this one is the battiest.

After all, science explains how the universe behaves. Religion suggests how *we* might.

Science has given us computers and vaccines, probed the recesses of the atom and the hinterlands of outer space. It is responsible for everything from anesthesia to supersonic travel to our understanding of quantum mechanics. New theories are tested experimentally every day. Some of them advance our knowledge. Those found wanting are rejected.

"If science proves some belief of Buddhism wrong," says the Dalai Lama, "then Buddhism will have to change. In my view, science and Buddhism share a search for truth and for understanding reality. By learning from science about aspects of reality where its understanding may be more advanced, I believe Buddhism enriches its own worldview."

Talk about enlightenment . . .

I'm not suggesting that science is without its shortcomings. You'll notice, for example, that while science can tell us how to build an atomic bomb, it doesn't address the somewhat significant question of whether to drop it on someone.

Science has everything to say about what is possible. It has nothing to say about what is permissible.

Clearly, that's one reason why Einstein remarked that, "Science without religion is lame, religion without science is blind."

Similarly, the late Stephen Jay Gould, an Alexander Agassiz Professor of Zoology and professor of geology at Harvard, argued that science and religion operate in entirely separate realms or, as he called them, "Non-Overlapping Magisteria."

"Science tries to document the factual character of the natural world, and to develop theories that coordinate and explain these facts," said Gould. "Religion, on the other hand, operates in the equally important, but utterly different realm of human purposes, meanings, and values—subjects that the factual domain of science might illuminate, but can never resolve . . . Science gets the age of rocks, and religion the rock of ages; science studies how the heavens go, religion how to go to heaven."

Some, however, would argue that science is uncovering so much about Nature that it is diminishing the majesty and mystery of life.

And while it's true that science has revealed a lot about our natural history, it is safe to assume that it will never explain how everything could have sprung from nothing. That leaves plenty of room for science to coexist with a genuine sense of spirituality.

After all, science doesn't contradict the universal values at the heart of religion. I have never heard a physicist or biologist argue against compassion . . . or forgiveness . . . or gratitude . . . or charity.

Moreover, many scientists and philosophers have written lucidly—even poetically—about the glories of creation.

The astronomer Carl Sagan said, "I would suggest that science is, at least in part, informed worship."

Eric Chaisson, author of *Cosmic Dawn,* writes that, "Without life, galaxies would twirl and stars would shine, but no one would appreciate the grandeur of it all."

The Austrian philosopher Ludwig Wittgenstein proclaimed that, "The mystical is not how the world is, but that it is."

Einstein wrote, "The most beautiful thing we can experience is the mysterious. It is the source of all true art and science. He to whom this emotion is a stranger, who can no longer pause to wonder and stand rapt in awe, is as good as dead: his eyes are closed."

And the Austrian philosopher of science Paul Feyerabend declared that a worthwhile life is not one devoted to scientific achievement, but to love. In the first draft of his autobiography, completed just before he died in 1994, he said love is what matters most. Without it, he said, "even the noblest achievements and the most fundamental principles remain pale, empty and dangerous."

Clearly, there is plenty of common ground here. If genuine scientific and religious principles oppose one another, perhaps it is only as your thumb opposes your fingers. Together you can use them to grasp the truth about life.

As the German poet and scientist Johann Wolfgang Von Goethe wrote a few hundred years ago, "The highest happiness of man . . . is to have probed what is knowable and quietly to revere what is unknowable." ∎

THE GREAT DISCONNECT

Surveys show that out of every ten Americans, nine believe in God, eight say that God is important to them personally, and more than seven report praying daily.

The United States is among the most religious nations on earth. But there is a great disconnect here. Consider a few sobering facts gleaned from Stephen Prothero's book *Religious Literacy*:

- Only half of Americans can name even one of the four gospels.
- The majority cannot name the first book of the Bible.
- Only one third know that it was Jesus who delivered the Sermon on the Mount.
- Most Americans don't know that Easter commemorates the resurrection.
- A majority wrongly believes that Jesus was born in Jerusalem.
- Most Americans do not know that the Trinity comprises the Father, Son, and Holy Spirit.
- The most widely quoted Bible verse in the United States—"The Lord helps those who helps themselves"—is not in the Bible.
- Ten percent of Americans believe Joan of Arc was Noah's wife.

Personally, I'm embarrassed for my fellow countrymen. Theologian David E. Wells says the Good Book is fast becoming "The Greatest Story Never Read." Historian R. Laurence Moore has a harsher assessment. He says Americans "are stupefyingly dumb about what they are supposed to believe."

Without some understanding of religion, how can we comprehend American history? The pilgrims risked their lives to come here and worship as they pleased. The American Revolution was launched with a declaration that men "are endowed *by their Creator* with certain inalienable rights." It was the doctrine of Manifest Destiny that propelled Americans westward. Even the Civil War was enveloped in religious controversy. Most southerners believed they were on the winning side of a theological argument. ("Slaves, obey your earthly masters with deep respect and fear. Serve them sincerely as you would serve Christ." Ephesians 6:5)

Without an understanding of religion, how can we grasp current events? Look at recent conflicts in Northern Ireland, the Middle East, or India and Pakistan. Each has religious underpinnings. When Osama bin Laden says his strategy is to engage "the crusader-Zionist alliance" in a clash of civilizations, most Americans don't even understand the reference.

Religion plays a major role in politics and policymaking in the United States today. Faith looms large in controversies over government funding of stem-cell research, abortion rights, creationism, and gay marriage.

At least minimal religious literacy is necessary to appreciate great music, literature, and art. What are we to make of the paintings of El Greco or Bach's sacred cantatas if we have no understanding of the religious beliefs of the era or the spiritual impulses of the artists?

How can we understand international culture without knowing something about the world's five major religions? Forget about understanding Buddhism's Four Noble Truths or the Five Pillars of Islam. Polls show the majority of Americans can't even name these two religions.

Prothero, the chair of the religion department at Boston University, observes that, "Americans are both deeply religious and profoundly ignorant about religion. . . . Here faith is almost entirely devoid of content. One of the most religious countries on earth is also a nation of religious illiterates."

What is the solution? Education. We can educate our children in our homes. We can teach them in our places of worship. But we should also teach something about religion in public schools.

Some will dismiss this as unconstitutional. But it's not.

As Prothero notes, the Supreme Court "has repeatedly and explicitly given a constitutional seal of approval to teaching about religion . . . [provided the crucial distinction is made] between theology and religious studies—between what Supreme Court Justice Arthur Goldberg called 'the teaching of religion' (which is unconstitutional) and 'the teaching about religion' (which is not)."

Most of us are sensible about this. After all, it is unlikely your third-grade teacher told you, "the pilgrims came to America to escape persecution. I can't tell you what kind."

Unfortunately, teaching much more than this *about* religion will not happen in most school districts. Teachers, principals, school boards, and textbook publishers simply don't want to wade into the firestorm.

Ironically, militant atheists—who don't want their children exposed to *any* religion—and fundamentalists—who don't want their children exposed to the *wrong* religion—have joined hands on this one.

However, nothing can stop us, or should stop us, from educating ourselves. As Marie Curie said, "Nothing in life is to be feared; it is only to be understood."   ∎

THE ATHEIST AND
THE APOLOGIST

Last year I had the honor of refereeing the "The Friday Night Fight" at Bally's in Las Vegas.

The two contenders?

In one corner, weighing in at a trim 142 pounds, was Dinesh D'Souza, a Robert and Karen Rishwain Fellow at the Hoover Institution at Stanford University and author of several best-selling books including, most recently, *What's So Great About Christianity.* Note the absence of a question mark. Mr. D'Souza is a Christian apologist.

In the other corner, weighing in at a brawny 174 pounds, was Christopher Hitchens, contributing editor of the *Atlantic Monthly* and *Vanity Fair* and also the author of several best-selling books including, most recently, *God Is Not Great: How Religion Poisons Everything.* Mr. Hitchens, as you may have surmised, is a confirmed atheist.

The debate was part of FreedomFest, billed as "The World's Largest Gathering of Free Minds." Over four days, we heard more than 70 speakers offer various views on investing, politics, history, religion, philosophy, science, medicine, and the arts.

This was the final debate of the conference. The resolution was: "War, Terrorism, and Geo-Political Crisis: Is Religion the Solution or the Problem?"

I told our two pugilists that while we expected a "spirited" debate—pardon the pun—we wanted this to be a fair fight, a clean fight. So I warned them that I would tolerate "no head butts, no ear-pulling, no eye-gouging, no biting, no slapping, no gagging, no faking an injury, no attacks to the windpipe, no neck cranks, no spine locks, no fish hooking, no hair-pulling, no groin strikes, no toe locks, no grabbing the throat, no punches to the head, no distracting the referee, no escaping the ring, and no unsportsmanlike conduct."

They both nodded in agreement, although Hitchens drew a laugh from the audience when he feigned a backhand to D'Souza's head on the way to the podium.

Over the next ninety minutes, the two combatants mesmerized the audience with provocative, enlightening, and frequently amusing arguments. D'Souza argued passionately that religion provides us with a set of values and an animating sense of purpose. Hitchens retorted that whatever benefits religion may provide, it is at the root of much of the intolerance, war, and terrorism that exists around the world today.

Few would disagree on these points. However, their other differences could not be reconciled, to put it mildly. A vote at the end of the debate showed the audience of 1,400 was pretty evenly split. (Hitchens conceded the victory to D'Souza, however, offering that he appeared to have won a slight majority.)

Afterwards, I joined Hitchens and D'Souza for dinner at Le Cirque across the street at Bellagio. I chuckled as I watched these two catch up on where they'd been, inquire about each other's families, and trade a few extra barbs.

Here were two men who had just been at each other's throats, whose views on religion could not be more opposite. Yet they genuinely like, admire, and respect each other.

Maybe there is a lesson here for the rest of us. Rather than focusing on our differences, perhaps we can search for common ground.

This is what Jeffrey Moses proposes in his book *Oneness: Great Principles Shared By All Religions.*

Moses points out that the world's spiritual truths are shared by all religions and by people of conscience everywhere. The Golden Rule is a good example:

Christianity—Do unto others as you would have them do unto you.

Judaism—What is hurtful to yourself do not to your fellow man. That is the whole of the Torah and the remainder is but commentary.

Islam—Do unto all men as you would wish to have done unto you; and reject for others what you would reject for yourselves.

Buddhism—Hurt not others with that which pains yourself.

Hinduism—This is the sum of all true righteousness—Treat others, as thou wouldst thyself be treated. Do nothing to thy neighbor, which hereafter thou wouldst not have thy neighbor do to thee.

Of course, some fanatical groups—not only today but throughout history—have ignored or subverted this universal truth. They have strayed—often in murderous ways—from their own principles. Yet as religion scholar Karen Armstrong has devoted her career to making clear, the essence of true religion is compassion:

Christianity—It is more blessed to give than to receive.

Taoism—Extend your help without seeking reward. Give to others and do not regret or begrudge your liberality.

Hinduism—Bounteous is he who gives to the beggar who comes to him in want of food and feeble.

Judaism—Blessed is he that considereth the poor.

Islam—The poor, the orphan, the captive—feed them for the love of God alone, desiring no reward, nor even thanks.

As Jeffrey Moses writes, "The great sayings are like a guide or blueprint for the inner development of mind and spirit that allows a person to achieve his highest goals. These principles are the foundation for success in personal relationships with family and friends, for satisfaction and success in business activities, and for that final aspiration in life that each person ultimately desires—the achievement of inner peace extending beyond the confines of an individual lifetime."

Of course, it is not enough to simply acknowledge this. We determine who we are not by what we believe, but by what we do. This simple truth is also found across the world's major religions:

Christianity—By their fruits ye may know them.

Hinduism—Students and teachers, and all others, who read the mere words of ponderous books, know nothing, but only waste their time in vain pursuit of words; he who acts righteously is wise.

Judaism—Not learning but doing is the chief thing.

Islam—A man asked Muhammad how to tell when one is truly faithful, and he replied: "If you derive pleasure from the good which you do and are grieved by the evil which you commit, then you are a true believer."

Buddhism—Like a beautiful flower, full of color, but without scent, are the fine but fruitless words of him who does not act accordingly.

"These great principles are not limiting to a person's satisfaction and fulfillment," says Moses. "Instead, they are guidelines that enable men and women to evolve to the highest point of human consciousness. . . . These principles stretch beyond time and change. They establish a clearly marked path which will enable each individual to attain the peace and enlightenment that is the ultimate goal in life."

More important than the sectarian beliefs that divide us are the great truths that unite us. And these truths have one overriding goal: right action.

An individual's actions cannot help but mirror what is in his mind. You need look no further than a man's behavior to see the extent of his inner development.

As the Dalai Lama observed, "Every major religion of the world has similar ideals of love, the same goal of benefiting humanity through spiritual practice, and the same effect of making their followers into better human beings."

As I witnessed in Las Vegas, even a devout believer and a militant atheist can respect each other, put their differences behind them, and enjoy each other's company.

So what's stopping the rest of us?   ■

GUIDEPOSTS ON THE FOOTPATH TO PEACE

The Seminole nation was forged in the 1700s, when Native Americans from Georgia, Alabama, and Mississippi joined up with the Creek Nation and African Americans who had escaped from slavery.

Unwilling to give up their land or way of life, the Seminole tribe fought a series of wars against the federal government in which more than 1,500 U.S. soldiers died. Eventually, the Seminoles won.

They still refer to themselves as America's "only unconquered Indian tribe," overcoming inhospitable wetlands, poverty, racism, and the military might of the U.S. government to gain independence and sovereignty.

Yes, Florida's Seminole Indian tribe has a proud history. But the present is another story.

Due to the success of its casino operations, the Seminoles have grown exceedingly wealthy, spending $965 million last year to purchase the Hard Rock International chain.

Each of the tribe's more than 3,300 members now gets free health care and college tuition—and everyone from infants to seniors receives monthly dividend checks that total more than $120,000 a year.

At first blush, it sounds like an incredible stroke of good fortune. But according to the *South Florida Sun Sentinel,* Seminole officials are concerned about "the alarming high-school dropout rate, drug and alcohol abuse, free-spending ways that can lead to unmanageable personal debt, and an erosion of the work ethic."

Former Tribal Chairman Howard Tommie says most families now have five or six cars, alongside airboats, motorcycles, all-terrain vehicles, and vacation homes. Yet the tribe is also dealing with an upsurge of young people killed in accidents and by drug overdoses. Many remain unemployed.

"The challenge for me and 90 percent of the tribe is motivation," says Louise Gopher, the Seminoles' education director. "Young people say, 'with so much money, why do I have to go to work, go to school.' It's like we've developed this monster. Now we have to deal with it."

Call it the downside of the dream. Millions of Americans long for sudden wealth. Many hope and pray for it.

But it wouldn't hurt to read John Steinbeck's novel *The Pearl* first.

An unexpected monetary windfall can alter your life in ways you might not imagine. Some people change their priorities or make bad decisions. Others lose sight of their long-held values. Still others discover they have attracted the wrong sort of people whom they mistakenly call friends.

Last year I played poker one evening with a money manager who handles the account of some lucky stiff who won the Florida State Lotto.

"He only won the jackpot about eight years ago," he told us. "But most of it is already gone. The rest won't take long at the rate he's going through it. And his life is a mess," he said shaking his head. "You wouldn't wish it on your worst enemy."

The problem isn't just sudden, unexpected wealth, like an inheritance or lottery win, coming to folks who aren't prepared for it. People who follow excellent, long-term habits of industry can also lose sight of what's important.

As B. C. Forbes wrote in his magazine in 1917, "Too many so-called 'successful' men are making business an end and aim in itself. They regard the multiplying of their millions and the extension of their works as the be-all and end-all of life. Such men are sometimes happy in a feverish, hustling sort of way, much as a fly placed in a tube of oxygen is furiously happy until its life burns out. But they have no time for the tranquil, finer, deeper joys of living. They are so obsessed with the material that they cannot enjoy the immaterial, the tangible, the ideal, the spiritual—quiet thought, self-communion, reflection, poise, inward happiness, domestic felicity. What profiteth it a man to gain uncounted riches if he thereby sacrifices his better self, his nobler qualities of manhood? Mere getting is not living."

I'm not a moon-eyed idealist who believes that money doesn't matter. It does. But an individual who is driven by his lust for "more" is hardly different than the donkey who is propelled onward by a carrot dangling at the end of a stick.

The secret is balance. Pursue your financial ambitions. But take time, too, to appreciate your health, your family, your friends, and the extraordinary world around you.

As clergyman Henry van Dyke wrote nearly 100 years ago, "To be glad of life, because it gives you the chance to love and to work and to play and to look up at the stars; to be satisfied with your possessions, but not contented with yourself until you have made the best of them; to despise nothing in the world except falsehood and meanness, and to fear nothing except cowardice; to be governed by your admirations rather than by your disgusts; to covet nothing that is your neighbor's except his kindness of heart and gentleness of manners; to think seldom of your enemies and often of your friends . . . these are little guideposts on the footpath to peace."   ∎

Two Great Thinkers on "The Good Life"

What does it mean to live a good human life?

Mankind has grappled with this question for thousands of years. But social scientist Charles Murray, co-author of the controversial bestseller *The Bell Curve,* argues that we're not thinking about it enough today.

At a recent lecture, he told the audience that one of the problems with education today is that students are no longer taught the difference "between being nice and being good."

Having spent much of the last two decades on college campuses, he observes that students "are not sexist, racist or homophobic. In conversation, they are earnest about social problems. They want to be generous to those who are less fortunate. They say please and thank you. But," he concludes, "being nice is not being good."

He proposes that we do a better job of educating our students about what *good* means as it applies to virtue, and *the Good* as a way of thinking about how to best live our lives.

Some might argue that this is the role of religion or the family. And in some households it is. But in many others it is not. And since public schools steer a wide berth when it comes to discussing the content of any faith, the educational system has become largely silent on this issue.

In his book *Real Education,* Murray points out that we can skirt sectarian controversy—and better prepare students for the future decisions they will have to make—by studying the core values of the world's great wisdom traditions, including those put forward by the Greek philosopher Aristotle and the great Chinese thinker Confucius.

Why should we listen to them? Because at some point in their lives, most thinking people realize that they will never achieve their youthful fantasies of money, power, or fame.

Nor will we live a life of unceasing adventure, circumnavigating Africa in a sailboat, feeling the tropical sun and ocean spray. (Film critic David Denby says the female version of this fantasy is Tuscany, "a primal paradise of sunshine, sex, love, terra-cotta tiles, and huge salads with real tomatoes.")

Aristotle reminds us that we should not be disappointed. Our final goal in life is not wealth (which is only a means to something else) or gratification (which he calls "the life for grazing animals").

Rather, he shows us that true happiness only results from living an active life in accordance with virtue. This notion seems decidedly out-of-touch in today's world.

Take sports, for example. Murray points out that we used to encourage our children to play sports so that they learned "fair play, courage in adversity, loyalty to teammates, modesty in victory, dignity in defeat."

Yet today we see professional athletes behaving like spoiled brats. Parents scream and swear at referees at Little League games. Coaches teach their players that "Winning isn't everything; it's the only thing" and "Show me a good loser and I'll show you a loser." Meanwhile, the media focuses on big contracts, multimillion dollar endorsements, and the celebrity lifestyle.

You don't hear much about virtue. The word itself sounds quaint, judgmental. Like you're out of sync with society's implied dictate to "do your own thing."

Aristotle reminds us that genuine contentment and lasting happiness don't come from fulfilling all our desires, but rather by reaching the highest levels of understanding and exercising virtue in our daily lives. This requires work—and practice.

In every area of life, our behavior quickly becomes habitual. A good habit becomes a virtue. A bad habit becomes a vice. (We've all known individuals whose uncontrolled appetites—bad habits—destroyed their lives.)

According to Aristotle, peace of mind is only achieved through reason, temperance, and noble character. Not easy. But the end result is a life lived in harmony, like a beautiful work of art.

Writing two centuries earlier, Confucius reached the same conclusion. Like Aristotle, he emphasized that the possession of virtue is not just a matter of recognizing the difference between right and wrong, but acting—living your life—in accordance with what you know to be right.

Murray asks, "If your children grow up to be courageous, temperate, able to think clearly about the consequences of their actions, to be concerned with the welfare of others, with a sense of obligation to set a good example for others in their own behavior and to accord to others their rightful due, do you really care whether they were raised to be good Aristotelians or Confucians?"

(Or, we might reasonably ask, good Christians or Buddhists or Muslims?)

At some point in our lives, most of us have thought—at least haphazardly—about the pursuit of the good life. But many have done it unaided.

"The problem," says Murray, is that we "have been given no help in tapping the magnificent body of thought on these issues that *homo sapiens* has already produced."

We should study the great wisdom traditions, he says, for one simple reason: *Being virtuous is hard.*

We face tough choices. Do you stay in a lousy marriage for the benefit of the kids? Do you move your aging father into a nursing home? Do you work harder to advance your career or spend more time with your family? Do you provide financial aid to your adult kids or let them struggle like you did?

How we answer important questions like these determines the course and quality of our lives. The decisions generally require trade-offs between short-term and long-term effects, costs and benefits, plusses and minuses.

We want to choose wisely. And after more than two millennia, Confucius and Aristotle still offer us practical solutions. They help us define and experience "the good life."

Of course, no philosophy, no ethical system, no religious faith has cornered the market on wisdom. So it behooves us to learn what we can from all the world's great traditions.

And, perhaps most importantly, never stop wrestling with the questions themselves.   ■

THE FORMULA FOR RE-ENCHANTMENT

Last spring, I spoke at an investment conference in Lake Tahoe.

If you've never been there, do yourself a favor and put it on your To-Do List. It's one of the most gorgeous places I've ever visited.

One Saturday afternoon, for instance, a few of my colleagues and I hiked the canyon trail up to Shirley Lake. With the weather warming up, the snow on the peaks was rapidly melting. That means the waterfalls were enormous—and spectacular.

Two and a half miles up we reached the huge granite face known as the RockPile, behind which looms Squaw Peak. The view down the valley from here is breathtaking.

Too bad more people weren't around to enjoy it. We only passed about one hiker every half hour.

On Sunday, we drove around to the eastern side of the lake where there is virtually no development. We took an easy beach trail along the shoreline to Skunk Harbor. The scenery is almost beyond description.

Imagine the snow-capped Sierra Nevada rising up over 6,000 feet from the clearest, bluest lake you've ever seen. And the weather was perfect, 65 degrees and not a cloud in the skies.

Yet, even though it was Sunday, we only saw two other hikers the whole afternoon. We were a week or two ahead of the peak season. But I think there's another explanation.

According to a study conducted by The Nature Conservancy and published by the National Academy of Sciences last year, people worldwide are giving Mother Nature the cold shoulder and spending more time indoors.

Thanks largely to "videophilia"—the love of sedentary activities involving electronic media—the typical American now spends 25 percent less time in nature than in 1987.

This is unfortunate for a couple of reasons. Number one, it's hard to imagine people feeling strongly about conserving our natural heritage if they can't be bothered to get outside and enjoy it.

Second, scientists say that getting out of our everyday artificial environment promotes mental health. For example, Dr. Howard Frumkin of Emory University Rollins School of Public Health has found that exposure to the natural environment actually prevents and helps treat certain illnesses. Furthermore, studies show that "videophilia" is contributing to obesity, lack of socialization, attention disorders, and poor academic performance.

Personally, I don't think there's a better way to spend an afternoon than tramping through the woods, the scent of earth and pine in the air, and not a sound to be heard but the rustling of the leaves and the sound of your own footsteps. No phones ringing. No horns honking. No television blaring.

How can you put a value on a few hours in the woods with nothing pressing to do and nowhere in particular to be? The combination of exercise, fresh air, and solitude is unbeatable. And it's invigorating.

Naturalist E. O. Wilson says, "To the extent that each person can feel like a naturalist, the excitement of the untrammeled world is regained. I offer this as a formula of re-enchantment."

Henry David Thoreau wrote that, "Nature is full of genius, full of the divinity."

Architect Frank Lloyd Wright agreed. "Nature is my manifestation of God. I go to nature every day for inspiration in the day's work."

So put on some comfortable shoes and get outside. There are plenty of easy trails out there, even if you huff and puff on two flights of stairs. Spending time in the Great Outdoors is exhilarating—and the ultimate stress reliever.

A couple years ago, I was spending the summer with my family in the Shenandoah Valley. But it was a working vacation—and I was up to my eyeballs in deadlines, projects, and conference calls. One afternoon, on sheer impulse, I grabbed my daughter Hannah, who was 8 at the time, and told her we were going up the Skyline Drive to White Oak Canyon, one of the best waterfall hikes in the Shenandoah National Park.

We threw some binoculars and a couple of peanut butter and jelly sandwiches into a backpack and headed out. Two hours later, we were sitting at the bottom of the falls, nibbling on our sandwiches, our bare feet dangling in the water.

We were alone, except for a curious chipmunk, some crayfish scuttling along the bottom of the pool, and a noisy kingfisher on a branch overhead. Hannah, who loves to hike, was drinking it all in, looking around at the falls, down at the water, and then up at the wind in the trees.

After a few minutes of contemplation, she looked up and asked with the sincerity that only an 8-year-old can muster, "Daddy, can we do this *every* day?"

I know I'll never forget that moment. Or how much I wanted to say yes. ∎

In Praise of Lifelong Learning

Last year I experienced heaven on earth. My family and I spent a week at the Chautauqua Institution.

Founded in 1874, the Institution is a nonprofit, 783-acre educational center on Chautauqua Lake in Southwestern New York State. Approximately 7,500 people are in residence here during the nine-week season from June to August. (Roughly 150,000 more will attend scheduled public events.)

The institution is not only a forum for open discussions on international relations, politics, religion, and science; it also promotes the arts with its own special studies programs, symphony orchestra, chamber group, and theater, ballet, and opera companies.

The institution sponsors daily lectures from prominent writers, artists, historians, diplomats, and scientists—either at the 5,000-seat open-air Amphitheater or at the Hall of Philosophy next door. And there are beautiful grounds that offer endless opportunities to run, bike, swim, fish, or boat.

Historian David McCullough, a frequent visitor to Chautauqua, said, "There is no place like it. No resort. No spa. Not anywhere else in the country, or anywhere else in the world. It is at once a summer encampment and a small town, a college campus, an arts colony, a music festival, a religious retreat and the village square—and there's no place—no place—with anything like its history."

Susan B. Anthony argued for women's suffrage here in 1892. FDR gave his "I Hate War" speech here in 1936. Over the years, Chautauqua has hosted thousands of prominent speakers, from Amelia Earhart and Thurgood Marshall to Kurt Vonnegut and Bill Cosby.

Why do they come? To help celebrate Chautauqua's ideal of lifelong learning.

Many of us apply ourselves in school and later strive to learn as much as we can about our business. But beyond that, education is often considered frivolous.

That's unfortunate. The more knowledge you possess, the more aware you are of our history and what is happening in the world, the richer your life becomes.

Lifelong learning broadens your horizons and expands your viewpoint. It enables you to make better decisions in both your business and personal life. And it's fun.

On a panel with publisher Steve Forbes, author Jeremy Siegel, and former Columbia University professor John Whitney at FreedomFest in Las Vegas two weeks earlier, we got into a discussion of the value of education beyond formal schooling.

I made the offhand remark that I don't care if my daughter Hannah—now 11—decides she wants to spin a pottery wheel for a living, as long as she is an *educated* pottery spinner.

The audience laughed, assuming I was kidding. I wasn't.

Like most parents, I want two primary things for my kids: health and happiness. If spinning pottery makes my daughter truly happy, that's what I hope she does.

Like the rest of us, however, she'll still need critical thinking skills and a high level of cultural literacy to make good choices and maximize her opportunities in life.

As John Adams said just before the American Revolution, "I must study politics and war, that my sons may have liberty to study mathematics and philosophy, navigation and commerce . . . in order to give their children a right to study paintings, poetry, music, architecture, statuary, tapestry and porcelain."

This was the upward climb the Founders envisioned for the good society. And you don't need 19 years of school or a visit to the Chautauqua Institution to experience it.

Like-minded people from New York to Los Angeles, for example, are signing up for One Day University, where award-winning professors from Harvard, Yale, Brown, Princeton, Dartmouth, Columbia, Cornell, and other top-tier schools come together for a single day to create a live classroom experience. One Day University bills itself as "The Best Professors from the Finest Schools, teaching their Greatest Courses."

If your schedule won't allow you to attend lectures, visit The Teaching Company online. It offers over 200 courses on history, philosophy, science, mathematics, economics, and literature in both CD and DVD formats. I've bought several of these courses and found them uniformly excellent.

If you go for a walk or run with your iPod, instead of listening to Jimmy Buffett for the umpteenth time, you can learn about the history of numbers, ancient Greek civilization, great American Broadway musicals, or the natural history of the earth.

There are also thousands of courses you can now take online, whether you want to earn a degree or just take a continuing education class.

However, you don't have to go online, attend a class, or spend a dime to make a commitment to lifelong learning. You can take full advantage of a fabulous 2,000-year old technology—the book—at your local library.

Not a bad idea, either. How can we make sound judgments or live our lives fully if our minds have not been opened and enlarged by reading, listening, and experiencing life broadly?

As Albert Einstein pointed out, "Learning is not a product of schooling but the lifelong attempt to acquire it."   ■

THE MYSTERIUM
TREMENDUM . . .
AND YOU

The other night I listened to a lecture by physicist Lawrence Krauss and was dismayed to hear his comments on scientific literacy in this country.

For example, when asked a straightforward true/false question about whether the earth revolves around the sun and takes one year to do so, half of respondents polled consistently get it wrong.

As an amateur astronomer (10-inch Meade Schmidt-Cassegrain for kindred spirits), I find this distressing. Too many of us know next to nothing about the universe we live in.

If your neighbor doesn't know the earth revolves around the sun, she probably isn't aware that our planet is spinning on its axis at over 1,000 miles per hour and traveling through space at 67,000 miles per hour, covering over a million and a half miles a day.

She's even less likely to know that the sun itself—and its retinue of planets—is orbiting the center of the Milky Way galaxy at a hair-raising 558,000 miles per hour. (We're just hitchhikers on for a brief ride.) Yet even at this speed, the sun takes approximately 225 million years to complete a single revolution.

Why so long? Because the Milky Way is bigger than our brains can imagine. Light, traveling 186,000 miles per second, takes 100,000 years to cross our galaxy.

Moreover, the Milky Way itself is traveling at roughly 660,000 miles per hour (and you wonder why you always feel rushed), gravitationally attracted to the Virgo cluster of galaxies. The Virgo Supercluster, in turn, is attracted to an even larger assembly of galaxies, the Great Attractor.

(Just so we're on the same page, the Great Attractor is a gravitation anomaly in intergalactic space, not Angelina Jolie.)

Like most galaxies, the Milky Way is mostly empty space. But it is home to over 200 billion stars. These stars, of course, are simply other suns. Every galaxy has billions of suns. And a recent Hubble Space Telescope image indicates there are over 240 billion galaxies in the visible universe.

The next time you go outside and look up at the twinkling lights—assuming you don't live near Broadway and 52nd—consider that there are more stars in the known universe than grains of sands on all the beaches on earth. (Billions and billions, indeed.)

Earth itself is orbiting a fairly ordinary star, a medium-size yellow dwarf. Beginning in October 1995, however, astronomers began discovering planets outside our solar system orbiting other stars. So far more than 300 of these "extrasolar" planets have been discovered, leading scientists to conclude that there are probably hundreds of billions—if not trillions—of planets out there.

Do any of them contain life? No one knows. But if extraterrestrial life exists, it is almost certainly weirder than anything having a drink at the Mos Eisley Cantina in *Star Wars*.

(As the English Astronomer Sir Arthur Eddington famously said, "Not only is the universe stranger than we imagine, it is stranger than we *can* imagine.")

Cosmologists estimate the universe is 156 billion light-years wide and 13.7 billion years old. How do they know these things? Through evidence, reason, and experimentation. Or, more specifically, by observing and measuring the redshifts of galaxies, the abundance of light elements, and the cosmic background radiation in the heavens.

Much about the universe remains beyond human comprehension, however. As H. L. Mencken said, "Penetrating so many secrets, we cease to believe in the unknowable. But there it sits, nevertheless, calmly licking its chops."

When asked what happened before the Big Bang, for example, physicist Stephen Hawking replies that the question is tantamount to asking "what lies north of the north pole?"

Some things we just don't know—and probably never will.

Yet it's worth remembering that everyone who lived and died before the 20th century never had good answers to these big questions about the universe. They looked up at night and wondered. They speculated. They told each other myths. But they didn't know.

Yet now that science has finally got it right, millions haven't bothered to learn.

Richard Dawkins, the first holder of the Charles Simonyi Chair for the Public Understanding of Science at the University of Oxford, writes that, "After sleeping through a hundred million centuries we have finally opened our eyes on a sumptuous planet, sparkling with color, bountiful with life. Within decades we must close our eyes again. Isn't it a noble, an enlightened way of spending our brief time in the sun, to work at understanding the universe and how we have come to wake up in it?"

The men and women who have visited space certainly have strong opinions on the subject. Many describe it as a near-mystical experience.

Astronaut James Irwin said, "The earth reminded us of a Christmas tree ornament hanging in the blackness of space. As we got farther and farther away it diminished in size. Finally it shrank to the size of a marble, the most beautiful marble you can imagine. That beautiful, warm, living object looked so fragile, so delicate, that if you touched it with a finger it would crumble and fall apart. Seeing this has to change a man . . . "

After returning from the moon, Neil Armstrong said, "I believe every human has a finite number of heartbeats. I don't intend to waste any of mine."

Space exploration has much to offer us, the earthbound majority. It inspires us. It teaches us brotherhood and humility. It reveals the connection between us and everything else that exists, reminding us of our place in the tapestry of creation. It provides us with a sense of wonder, a feeling of awe.

In fact, much of what we understand about the cosmos dovetails with Rudolph Otto's characteristics of religious experience: the holy; the sacred; gratitude and oblation; thanksgiving; awe before the *mysterium tremendum*; the sense of the divine; the ineffable; the quality of exaltedness and sublimity; powerlessness; the impulse to surrender and to kneel; a sense of the eternal; fusion with the universe as a whole.

These experiences are open to anyone who looks up at night, believers and nonbelievers alike.

As astronomer Carl Sagan wrote in *Pale Blue Dot:*

> Our planet is a lonely speck in the great enveloping cosmic dark. In our obscurity, in all this vastness, there is no hint that help will come from elsewhere to save us from ourselves. It is up to us. It's been said that astronomy is a humbling, and, I might add, a character-building experience. To my mind, there is perhaps no better demonstration of the folly of human conceits than this distant image of our tiny world. To me, it underscores our responsibility to deal more kindly and compassionately with one another and to preserve and cherish that pale blue dot, the only home we've ever known. ∎

My Kind of Martyr

The assassins' bomb went off at 12:50 P.M. with a blinding flash and a deafening bang.

Everyone in the room was thrown to the floor, eardrums pierced. Some were dead. Others were severely injured by shrapnel, flying pieces of wood and other debris. Pockets and boots were full of glass. Everyone's hair stood up from the suction and heat of the explosion. The intended victim, however, was largely unharmed.

The date was July 20, 1944. The target was Adolph Hitler.

At the time, the attempt on the life of the Fuhrer raised profound ethical questions among some German theologians.

Dietrich Bonhoeffer was not one of them.

Born in 1906 to a prominent professor of psychiatry and neurology and one of the few women of her generation to obtain a university degree, Bonhoeffer was a precocious boy. At 10, he was playing Mozart piano sonatas. By 21, he had earned a doctorate in theology.

Raised in a household indifferent to religion, Bonhoeffer shocked his family at age 14 when he announced his intention to become a pastor and theologian.

His older brother Karl-Friedrich, who later became a distinguished physicist, tried to talk him out of it, arguing that the church was weak, silly, irrelevant, and unworthy of a young man's lifelong commitment.

"If the church really is what you say it is," Dietrich replied, "then I will have to reform it."

As a young man, he traveled to the United States in the early 1930s, recognized the plight of minorities, and worked among impoverished blacks in Harlem. He traveled to India to study nonviolent resistance under Gandhi.

As Hitler rose to power, however, Bonhoeffer became upset that Germany's Protestant church—shaped by nationalism and obedience to the state—supported the maniacal dictator.

Bonhoeffer spoke out openly against Hitler's anti-Semitism. The Gestapo reacted by banning him from preaching, then teaching, and finally any kind of public speaking.

In 1943, Bonhoeffer was arrested for helping several Jews escape Germany through Switzerland. He was later released.

But when his involvement in the plot to kill Hitler was uncovered, he was quickly apprehended and sentenced to death.

During his incarceration, Bonhoeffer voiced frustration with his church through numerous papers and letters. He felt that in choosing between its principles and its survival, the German Lutheran church had opted for the latter.

Bonhoeffer began advocating what he called "religionless Christianity." He argued that genuine spirituality is about action not words, that what we do is infinitely more important than what we believe.

"If you board the wrong train," he said, "it is no use running along the corridor in the other direction."

After his arrest, Bonhoeffer was moved from one concentration camp to another, ending at Flossenburg. Fellow captives described how he aided and consoled them right up until the end.

Bonhoeffer was executed eleven days before the liberation of Flossenburg, less than a month before the fall of Berlin.

It would be comforting to imagine that such a gentle soul experienced a relatively quick and painless death. This was not the case.

According to Wikipedia, "Like other executions associated with the July 20 Plot, the execution was brutal. Bonhoeffer was stripped of his clothing, tortured and ridiculed by the guards, and led naked into the execution yard. A lack of sufficient gallows to hang the plotters caused Hitler and Nazi propagandist Josef Goebbels to use meathooks from slaughterhouses to slowly hoist the victim by a noose formed of piano wire. Asphyxiation is thought to have taken half an hour."

Bonhoeffer was 39.

By any measure, the life of this Lutheran minister was extraordinary. He took enormous risks. He wrangled with his church, eventually leaving it to found another.

He struggled with his conscience, telling the Bishop of Chichester in neutral Sweden that through the German Resistance movement he feared he was "sacrificing his righteousness."

But he asked his followers to contrast cheap grace with costly grace. Costly grace, he said, is grace that impels action.

Philosopher Daniel Dennett concurs. In *Breaking the Spell,* he writes, "There are many people who quite innocently and sincerely believe that if they are earnest in attending to their own personal 'spiritual' needs, this amounts to living a morally good life. I know many activists, both religious and secular, who agree with me: these people are deluding themselves."

True religion, Bonhoeffer argued, is not about meditation, fine sentiments, or heartfelt prayers. It is first and foremost about following the dictates of conscience—and taking action.

Some may find it odd to canonize a young pastor who flouted authority, abandoned his church, and helped plot an assassination.

The world we live in, however, is not always a neat and tidy one. People, government—and religious institutions—can disappoint.

Our challenge is to do the right thing anyway.

"The ultimate test of a moral society," said Bonhoeffer, "is the kind of world that it leaves to its children." ■

FINDING MEANING IN AN AGE OF DOUBT

Two years ago, at a conference at Chateau D'Ermeonville—an agreeable old pile of stones about thirty miles north of Paris—I shared some investment counsel with a group of investors.

The advice wasn't exactly cutting-edge. It was 300 years old.

We were on a cultural tour of France at the time and my topic that day was "Voltaire on Investing."

Born in 1694, Voltaire was a French poet, dramatist, historian, satirist, philosopher, and writer of masterpieces of fiction, such as *Candide.*

He was an early advocate of free trade, civil liberties, and freedom of religion. Indeed, his shadow is so long that the French Enlightenment itself is known as "The Age of Voltaire."

He was an exceedingly wealthy man, too—a millionaire before the age of 40. (And this, as they say, was back when a million francs really *meant* something.)

Voltaire began his business career by cultivating a friendship with two brothers in Paris who had a contract to supply the French army with food and munitions.

Yet he scored a real coup in 1728 when a mathematician friend informed him that the French government had authorized a lottery in which the prize was much greater than the collective cost of the tickets. Voltaire organized a syndicate, bought every possible combination, and, of course, collected the prize. He then used this capital to become a moneylender to the Great Houses of Europe.

As a businessman and investor, Voltaire was no slouch. But what can he teach us three centuries later?

Voltaire had a highly skeptical nature. So do most of the world's great investors.

They understand that no one can accurately and consistently predict the economy and financial markets. This is especially important to bear in mind today as we muddle through an economic crisis of unprecedented origin.

Voltaire's skepticism, however, ranged far beyond business and investment matters. He was skeptical of the revealed truth of the Church, skeptical of the divine right of kings, skeptical of the wealth and position of the aristocracy, skeptical of the "wisdom" of the common man.

Defending his doubts in both his writings and debates, Voltaire became known as "The Voice of the Enlightenment." And his incredulous approach has often been considered a hallmark of wisdom.

Euripides said a man's most valuable trait is a judicious sense of what not to believe.

Rene Descartes said, "If you would be a real seeker of the truth, it is necessary that at least once in your life you doubt, as far as possible, all things."

Psychologist Erich Fromm argued that the quest for certainty blocks the quest for meaning.

H. L. Mencken took a more extreme view. "We are here and it is now. Further than that, all human knowledge is moonshine."

Society, of course, practically demands that we maintain a skeptical attitude. Advertisements make outlandish claims. Convicts insist they are innocent. Political candidates promise the moon. The car salesman insists the previous owner was a little old lady who only drove it to church on Sundays.

Skepticism becomes our chain mail suit. And in an age dominated by science and reason, our doubts have carried over to spiritual matters, too.

Many thoughtful men and women today are uncomfortable with both religious fundamentalism and the postmodern abdication of faith. Some argue that spiritual poverty has replaced material poverty as the leading want in the West.

Millions struggle to find meaning in an age of doubt. Yet the quest might begin by acknowledging something about which we can be quite certain: You are bound to everyone alive today by ties of genealogical descent. In the most literal sense, we are all cousins, sharing what Voltaire called "a point between two eternities."

"Strange is our situation here on Earth," wrote Albert Einstein. "Each of us comes for a short visit, not knowing why, yet sometimes seeming to divine a purpose. From the standpoint of daily life, however, there is one thing we do know: that man is here for the sake of other men—above all for those whose smiles and well-being our own happiness depends."

Yet great suffering persists . . .

In the twentieth century alone, at least 60 million people were killed by war, more than the total number of people alive when Moses reputedly wandered the Sinai. The World Bank estimates that 1.4 billion people live in destitution today, seven times the total number of men and women alive worldwide when Jesus walked the dirt byways of the Promised Land, preaching clemency for the poor.

In Darfur, more than 2 million people have been driven from their homes, creating one of the world's worst humanitarian crises.

In Congo, more than 5.4 million have died in war since 1998. 45,000 are still dying each month, mostly from nonviolent causes such as malaria, pneumonia, and malnutrition—easily preventable and treatable conditions.

In Somalia, more than 1.9 million—35 percent of the population—are in urgent need of food and medical assistance.

In Iraq, more than 2 million people have been uprooted by sectarian violence. Many are living in Jordan or Syria. They have no legal status and many of them are desperate for food, medicine, jobs, and a safe place to live.

In Zimbabwe—aside from its many political and economic problems—there is a cholera epidemic. Millions lack access to safe water, food, and the most basic sanitation and health services.

In the face of such overwhelming suffering, it is natural for some to feel that there is nothing they can do but pray.

Not so. You can donate something—anything—to great humanitarian organizations like Doctors Without Borders or the International Rescue Committee.

Helping others—especially those in greatest need—is among life's most rewarding experiences. Moreover, it is guaranteed to create purpose in your life.

In *Beside Still Waters: Searching for Meaning in an Age of Doubt,* Gregg Easterbrook writes:

> In the ancient desert, people who by our standards possessed nothing of value and understood little of the world nevertheless learned to give their lives meaning by embracing spiritual dreams of love and justice. They found higher purpose where it has always been and will always be, within the heart. In this, anyone may believe. ■

Renewing a Forgotten Virtue

What would you most like to leave to your kids some day? A house . . . a business . . . some money?

If so, there is plenty of good advice out there about what to do and how to do it. A good starting point, in my view, is Warren Buffett's suggestion to leave your children enough money so that they could do what they want, but not so much that they could do nothing.

There are more important things we can leave them, however. Plato said, "Let parents bequeath to their children not riches, but the spirit of reverence."

Reverence means understanding human limitations. It's a feeling of respect and awe about what lies beyond our control: time, nature, truth, fate, death.

It's also an attitude of acceptance toward life and our fellow human beings, flawed as we may be. Reverence underlies the grace and civility that make life in society bearable and pleasant. It reminds us what's important, what's sacred, what's worth protecting.

Reverence is as old as civilization itself, perhaps older. Writing in the fifth and fourth centuries B.C.E., the Greek historian Thucydides called it a cardinal virtue, existing universally across all cultures.

An irreverent man, he claimed, is arrogant and shameless, full of hubris, unable to feel awe in the face of things greater than himself. Moreover, irreverence makes it difficult to respect those who are weaker: children, prisoners, the poor, the elderly.

Many equate reverence with religiosity. Yet this is not always the case.

In *Reverence: Renewing a Forgotten Virtue,* Paul Woodruff writes:

> Reverence is not faith, because the faithful may hold their faith with arrogance and self-satisfaction, and the reverent may not know what to believe . . . If your form of worship or faith is reverent, so much the better. You know one place to look for reverence. But you should look further, so that you can see how you might share reverence with people who do not worship with you or share your faith.

Throughout history, religion and reverence have often gone their separate ways. Taken to extremes, religious beliefs sometimes engender just the opposite: intolerance, guilt, fear, ignorance, zealotry, and hatred.

In the West today, however, most of us live peaceably beside those with different beliefs. What the devout admire in other religions, however, is not faith, since they reject most of its content, but rather reverence, that universal sense of awe, respect, and humility.

Some experience reverence in organized worship, in community with others. Others discover it outdoors, enjoying the glories of nature. Still others may experience it with music.

Handel's *Messiah,* Mendelssohn's *St. Paul* oratorio, Bach's *Mass in B Minor,* and many other classical and choral masterpieces were clearly inspired by a deep sense of reverence—and, centuries later, still bring that spirit forth.

Yet something else comes closer to capturing the true spirit of reverence: silence.

"Do you imagine the universe is agitated?" asked Lao Tzu a few thousand years ago. "Go into the desert at night and look at the stars. This practice should answer the question."

A quiet mind, freed from a noisy environment and the onslaught of continuous thought, has long been a signpost of spiritual development.

In Christianity and Judaism, there is the silence of contemplative prayer. In Islam, the Sufis wrote about the wisdom of finding silence within. Hinduism, the source of yoga, emphasizes the importance of silence for inner growth. Buddhists believe that silent meditation is the path to enlightenment. For Quakers, silence makes up much of the service, allowing for the development of heart and mind.

Secular philosophers and other writers have advocated its benefits, as well.

Transcendentalist Ralph Waldo Emerson said, "I like the silent church before the service begins better than any preaching."

Humanist Aldous Huxley observed that, "Silence is as full of potential wisdom and wit as the unhewn marble of great sculpture."

Claude Debussy even reminded listeners that music is found in the space between the notes. Avant-garde composer John Cage took this idea to an extreme. His composition *4′33″* consists of just over four and a half minutes of complete silence. (To this day, it's the only piece I can play on the violin.)

Silence opens us to the experience of reverence. Yet many today lead noisier lives than ever. Some choose to live near busy highways and airports. Restaurants and retail stores blast rock and country music nonstop. A study conducted by Pennsylvania State University found that urban teenagers listen to four and a half hours of pop and rap music a day. In our homes, radio and television broadcasts are punctuated with a steady stream of commercial messages at trumped up volumes.

This creates frustration and anxiety, especially for innocent bystanders. In *The Happiness Hypothesis,* psychology professor Jonathan Haidt writes that "noise, especially noise that is variable or intermittent, interferes with concentration and increases stress. It's worth striving to remove sources of noise in your life."

Sensible advice. Yet Matthew Kelly believes there is another reason we choose noisy environments: Silence reveals our weaknesses to us, our shortcomings.

In *The Rhythm of Life,* he writes, "In the silence, we see at one time the person we are and the person we are capable of becoming . . . . It is precisely for this reason that we fill our lives with noise, to distract ourselves from the challenge to change."

We can fix this, however. We can hit the off button, walk outside, visit a chapel, or take a quiet drive in the country. If you really can't escape the barking dogs, screaming kids, or NFL football, do yourself a favor and buy a pair of noise-canceling headphones. (Trust me, they're worth it.)

A few days ago, I took my 5-year-old son David on a hike up to Humpback Rocks, an outcropping about half a mile above the Blue Ridge Parkway that offers an awe-inspiring view of the Shenandoah Valley, especially near sunset.

As we approached the summit, I stopped and asked him to listen. "What do you hear?" I asked.

He looked around the trail and up at the treetops. There was no traffic, no sound, not even the wind. He shrugged and said, "nothing."

"Isn't it great?" I asked.

He glanced up to make sure I wasn't kidding then looked around again, listening.

"Yeah," he said, exhaling. "It is." ∎

The Secret of Shelter Island

"Annual income twenty pounds, annual expenditure nineteen nineteen six, result happiness," the novelist Charles Dickens wrote. "Annual income twenty pounds, annual expenditure twenty pounds ought and six, result misery."

If that's too literary for your taste, an article in the *New York Times* last year put a finer point on it:

> For more than half a century, Americans have proved staggeringly resourceful at finding new ways to spend money. . . . But now the freewheeling days of credit and risk may have run their course—at least for a while and perhaps much longer—as a period of involuntary thrift unfolds in many households. With the number of jobs shrinking, housing prices falling and debt levels swelling, the same nation that pioneered the no-money-down mortgage suddenly confronts an unfamiliar imperative: more Americans must live within their means.

I may hold a minority view, but this is probably a good thing.

Capitalism does a wonderful job of improving our standard of living, creating jobs, generating wealth, and offering us a spectacular and unending array of new products to lust after. But beware *too much* of a good thing.

In the continual pursuit of greater material success, some of us lose important relationships, our health, our perspective, our peace of mind. (And, perhaps even, our credit rating.)

Modern commercial culture often promotes a sense of lack, a constant, gnawing belief that something is missing. If only we had another car, a better car, a bigger house, a more lavish kitchen, a trip to St. Thomas—or whatever—*then* we would finally be set.

Unfortunately, life doesn't work that way. You can amass more and more stuff, yet find you're still not satisfied. You have no sense of abundance. Meanwhile, the bill collector is knocking at the door.

Psychologist Dr. Martin Seligman calls this getting caught on the "hedonic treadmill." In *Authentic Happiness* he writes, "As you accumulate more material possessions, your expectations rise. The things you worked so hard for no longer make you happy; you need to get something even better to boost your level of happiness. But once you get the next possession, you adapt to it as well, and so on. . . . If there were no treadmill, people who get more good things would in general be much happier than the less fortunate. But the less fortunate are, by and large, just as happy as the more fortunate."

The poet William Wordsworth got wise to this two hundred years ago. "Getting and spending," he wrote, "we lay waste our powers."

A few other bright guys have offered us essentially the same message. Including, perhaps, the smartest of them all: Albert Einstein. The Nobel Prize–winning physicist said, "The trite objects of human efforts—possessions, outward success, luxury— have always seemed to me contemptible. . . . I believe a simple and unassuming manner of life is best for everyone, best both for the body and the mind."

Not to mention the bank account.

Of course, material possessions aren't just a monetary consideration. Once you accumulate a bunch of stuff, you find you've created a whole new set of problems. You have to store it, care for it, maintain it, move it, insure it. Hence the old saying, "Do you own your possessions, or do they own you?"

Fortunately, no one is required to buy into the consumerist mentality. We can step off the hedonic treadmill whenever we want. We can choose to live more simply and forget about the Joneses. (They've already forgotten about you, by the way.)

In a society as rich as ours, a sense of lack is really just a state of mind.

Vanguard founder John Bogle has often told a story about a party given by a billionaire on Shelter Island:

"At the party, Kurt Vonnegut informs his pal, the author Joseph Heller, that their host, a hedge fund manager, had made more money in a single day than Heller had earned from his wildly popular novel *Catch-22* over its whole history. Heller responds, 'Yes, but I have something he will never have . . . *Enough.*'"   ■

AFTERWORD

What is the real secret of Shelter Island?

Money can buy freedom from want and from work that is drudgery. But beyond that, it begins losing its power.

Most certainly, it cannot buy contentment. The stark finding of recent studies is that beyond the safety net, more money adds little or nothing to your subjective well-being. Yet almost everywhere, people imagine it will.

We can spend decades chasing this dream only to be disappointed when we arrive. After all, who would rather be a wealthy coot than a young man roaming the boulevards of Paris with just a few euros in his pocket?

Aristotle had the right idea. Our target is the golden mean, the felicitous middle between the extremes of excess and deficiency. Buddhists call this "the Middle Way," the path between austerity and sensual indulgence. Perhaps it really does lead to enlightenment.

Beyond material comfort, our happiness is highly dependent on principle-centered living. To the extent that we abide by timeless, universal principles, we are happy, engaged, satisfied with our lot. To the extent that we depart from these principles, our conscience aches—or should—and trouble follows.

Recognizing this won't change a thing, however. As the proverb says, wisdom is knowing what to do next. Virtue is *doing it*.

■ ■ ■

Readers often ask what inspired me to write these essays. One reason was I wanted to share a few things I've learned over the past 50 years—and perhaps have a positive influence.

In *What Is Man?*, Mark Twain writes, "The chance reading of a book or of a paragraph in a newspaper, can start a man on a new track and make him renounce his old associations and seek new ones that are in sympathy with his new ideal; and the result for that man, can be an entire change of his way of life."

This is more than any sensible writer should expect, of course. Yet some of us remain insensible.

More than anything, I wanted to pass along a few ideas that I believe are essential to my kids, Hannah and David. That's why I dedicated this book to them.

They're too young to get most of this now. But I hate the thought of them learning *all* these lessons the hard way.

As a bonus, I like to imagine that one day they'll read a few pages, look up and say, "maybe Dad wasn't such a *blockhead* after all."

Fat chance, I know. Twain *also* said, "When I was a boy of fourteen, my father was so ignorant I could hardly stand to have the old man around. But when I got to be twenty-one, I was astonished by how much he'd learned in seven years."

Let me raise a glass in solidarity with parents everywhere who are still waiting for their children to receive this revelation.

For now, mine are too young. But perhaps some day a few words here will inspire or motivate them.

If so, I hope they *seize the day*.

BIBLIOGRAPHY

Allen, James. *As a Man Thinketh*. Los Angeles: DeVorss & Company, 1902.

Berry, Wendell. *The Pleasures of Eating*. New York: Farrar, Straus and Giroux, 1990.

Bloom, Harold. *Shakespeare: The Invention of the Human*. New York: Penguin, 1998.

Boaz, David. "Are We Freer?" *The Cato Policy Report*. Vol. XXXI, No. 1. Jan 2009.

Boldt, Laurence G. *The Tao of Abundance: Eight Ancient Principles for Living Abundantly in the 21st Century*. New York: Penguin, 1999.

Bowen, Will. *A Complaint Free World: How to Stop Complaining and Start Enjoying the Life You Always Wanted*. New York: Random House, 2007.

Branden, Nathaniel. *The Art of Living Consciously: The Power of Awareness to Transform Everyday Life*. New York: Fireside, 1999.

Bryson, Bill. *Shakespeare: The World as Stage*. New York: Harper-Collins, 2007.

Bryson, Bill. *A Short History of Nearly Everything.* New York: Random House, 2003.

Buffone, Gary. *The Myth of Tomorrow: Seven Essential Keys for Living the Life You Want Today.* New York: McGraw-Hill, 2002.

Campbell, Joseph. Ed. Diane K. Osbon. *Reflections on the Art of Living: A Joseph Campbell Companion.* New York: HarperCollins, 1995.

Chaisson, Eric. *Cosmic Dawn: The Origins of Matter and Life.* New York: Norton, 1989.

Collins, Billy. "Dharma." *Sailing Alone Around the Room: New and Selected Poems.* New York: Random House, 2002.

Covey, Steve. *Everyday Greatness: Inspiration for a Meaningful Life.* Nashville: Thomas Nelson, 2006.

Covey, Steve. *First Things First.* New York: Simon and Schuster, 1994.

Csikszentmihalyi, Mihaly. *Flow: The Psychology of Optimal Experience.* New York: HarperCollins, 1991.

cummings, e. e. "A Poet's Advice to Students." *E. E. Cummings, a Miscellany: A Miscellany.* New York: The Argophile Press, 1958.

Dalai Lama. *Ethics for the New Millennium.* New York: Penguin, 1999.

Dawkins, Richard. *Unweaving the Rainbow.* Boston: Houghton Mifflin, 1998.

Dennett, Daniel. *Breaking the Spell: Religion as a Natural Phenomenon.* New York: Viking, 2006.

Dowd, Maureen. "An Ideal Husband." *New York Times.* 6 July 2008.

Easterbrook, Gregg. *Beside Still Waters: Searching For Meaning In an Age of Doubt.* New York: HarperCollins, 1998.

Easterbrook, Gregg. "Life Is Good, So Why Do We Feel So Bad?" *Wall Street Journal.* 13 June 2008.

Easterbrook, Gregg. *The Progress Paradox: How Life Gets Better While People Feel Worse.* New York: Random House, 2003.

Emerson, Ralph Waldo. "What is Success?"

Epictetus. *The Art of Living: The Classic Manual on Virtue, Happiness, and Effectiveness.* New York: Harper, 2005.

Feyerabend, Paul. *Killing Time: The Autobiography of Paul Feyerabend.* Chicago: University of Chicago Press, 1996.

Florida, Richard. *Who's Your City?: How the Creative Economy Is Making Where to Live the Most Important Decision of Your Life.* New York: Basic Books, 2008.

Gilbert, Daniel. *Stumbling on Happiness.* New York: Random House, 2006.

Getty, J. Paul. *How to Be Rich.* New York: Penguin, 1965.

Gladwell, Malcolm. *Blink: The Power of Thinking Without Thinking.* New York: Hachette, 2005.

Goodman, Peter. "Economy Fitful, Americans Start to Pay as They Go." *New York Times.* 5 February 2008.

Gould, Stephen Jay. *Rock of Ages.* New York: Random House, 1999.

Heller, Erich. *The Disinherited Mind.* Harmondsworth: Penguin Books, 1961.

Hernstein, Richard and Charles Murray. *The Bell Curve: Intelligence and Class Structure in American Life.* New York: Simon and Schuster, 1996.

Hollis, James. *Finding Meaning in the Second Half of Life: How to Finally, Really Grow Up.* New York: Penguin, 2005.

Horgan, John. *Rational Mysticism: Spirituality Meets Science in the Search for Enlightenment.* New York: Houghton Mifflin Harcourt, 2004.

Jordan, Hamilton. *No Such Thing as a Bad Day.* Atlanta: Longstreet Press, 2001.

Jung, Carl. *Memories, Dreams, Reflections.* New York: Random House, 1963.

Karlgaard, Rich. "Godly Work." *Forbes.* April 23, 2007.

Keller, Helen. "Three Days to See." *Atlantic Monthly.* January 1933.

Kelly, Matthew. *The Rhythm of Life: Living Every Day with Passion and Purpose.* New York: Reed Elsevier, 2004.

Klein, Stefan. *The Secret Pulse of Time: Make Sense of Life's Scarcest Commodity.* New York: Da Capo Press, 2007.

Kornfield, Jack and Christina Feldman. *Soul Food: Stories to Nourish the Spirit and the Heart.* New York: Harper, 1996.

Lynch, Peter. *One Up On Wall Street: How to Use What You Already Know to Make Money in the Market.* New York: Penguin, 1990.

Maslow, Abraham H. *Motivation and Personality,* 3rd ed. 1954. Ed. Cynthia McReynolds. New York: Harper and Row, 1987.

Masterson, Michael. "How to Accomplish All Your Most Important Goals . . . Without Fail." *Early to Rise.* 25 February 2008. www.earlytorise.com/2008/02/25/using-daily-task-lists-to-accomplish-your-goals-2.html.

Maxwell, John C. *The Difference Maker: Making Your Attitude Your Greatest Asset.* New York: Thomas Nelson, 2006.

Maxwell, John C. *Today Matters: 12 Daily Practices to Guarantee Tomorrows Success.* New York: Hachette, 2004.

Mencken, H. L. *A Mencken Chrestomathy.* New York: Random House, 1982.

Moorhead, Hugh. *The Meaning of Life.* Chicago: Chicago Review Press, 1988.

Moses, Jeffrey. *Oneness: Great Principles Shared by All Religions.* New York: Random House, 1992.

Noonan, Peggy. "A Life's Lesson." *Wall Street Journal.* 20 June 2008.

O'Kelly, Eugene. *Chasing Daylight: How My Forthcoming Death Transformed My Life.* New York: McGraw-Hill, 2005.

O'Rourke, P. J. "Fairness, Idealism, and Other Atrocities." *Los Angeles Times.* 4 May 2008.

Percy, Walker. Foreword to John Kennedy Toole, *A Confederacy of Dunces.* New York: Grove, 1987.

Pollan, Michael. *In Defense of Food: An Eater's Manifesto.* New York: Penguin, 2008.

Pollan, Stephen M. and Mark Levine. *It's All in Your Head: Thinking Your Way to Happiness.* New York: HarperCollins, 2005.

Post, Stephen. *Why Good Things Happen to Good People: How the Simple Act of Giving Can Bring You a Longer, Happier, Healthier Life.* New York: Random House, 2008.

Prothero, Stephen. *Religious Literacy: What Every American Needs to Know—And Doesn't.* New York: Harper, 2007.

Robinson, Edwin Arlington. "Richard Cory." 1897.

Sagan, Carl. *Pale Blue Dot: A Vision of the Human Future in Space.* New York: Random House, 1997.

Sagan, Carl. *The Varieties of Scientific Experience: A Personal View of the Search for God.* New York: Penguin, 2006.

Schopenhauer, Arthur. "On the Foundations of Morality." 1839.

Schopenhauer, Arthur. *The Wisdom of Life.* New York: Dover, 1891.

Seligman, Martin. *Authentic Happiness: Using the New Positive Psychology to Realize Your Potential for Lasting Fulfillment.* New York: Simon and Schuster, 2002.

Shermer, Michael. *The Mind of the Market: Compassionate Apes, Competitive Humans, and Other Tales from Evolutionary Economics.* New York: Macmillan, 2007.

Shermer, Michael. *Why People Believe Weird Things: Pseudoscience, Superstition, and Other Confusions of Our Time.* New York: Holt, 2002.

Smith, Adam. *The Theory of Moral Sentiments.* London: A Millar, 1759.

Smith, Adam. *The Wealth of Nations.* 1776.

Skousen, Mark. *EconoPower: How a New Generation of Economists is Transforming the World.* Hoboken NJ: John Wiley & Sons, 2008.

Storr, Anthony. *Music and the Mind.* New York: Random House, 1993.

Templeton, John. *Discovering the Laws of Life.* West Conshohocken, PA: Templeton Foundation, 1994.

Templeton, John. *Wisdom from World Religions.* West Conshohocken, PA: Templeton Foundation, 2002.

Tolle, Eckhart. *A New Earth: Awakening to Your Life's Purpose*. New York: Dutton, 2005.

Tolle, Eckhart. *The Power of Now: A Guide to Spiritual Enlightenment*. Novato, CA: New World Library, 1999.

Tracy, Brian. *Goals: How to Get Everything You Want—Faster Than You Ever Thought Possible*. San Francisco: Berrett-Koehler Publishers, 2003.

Wayland, John W. "The True Gentleman." 1899.

Wilson, Edward O. *Biophilia*. Cambridge, MA: Harvard University Press, 1984.

Woodruff, Paul. *Reverence: Renewing a Forgotten Virtue*. New York: Oxford University Press, 2001.

Wordsworth, William. "The World is Too Much with Us." 1807.

Zweig, Jason. "The Depression of 2008? Don't Count on It." *Wall Street Journal*. 30 September 2008.

ABOUT THE AUTHOR

Alexander Green is the Investment Director of The Oxford Club, Chairman of Investment U, editor of *Spiritual Wealth* and author of the *New York Times* bestseller *The Gone Fishin' Portfolio: Get Wise, Get Wealthy . . . and Get On With Your Life.*

Alex has been featured on CNBC, Fox Television and *The O'Reilly Factor*, and has been profiled in the *Wall Street Journal*, *BusinessWeek*, *Forbes*, *Kiplinger's Personal Finance*, and many other publications.

He currently lives near Charlottesville, Virginia, with his wife, Karen, and their children, Hannah and David.

Websites:

www.oxfordclub.com

www.investmentu.com

www.spiritualwealth.com

Email: oxford@oxfordclub.com

INDEX

Special Offer for

The Secret of Shelter Island Readers

Get a **47% discount** on a membership to
Alexander Green's investment letter,
The Oxford Club Communiqué.

As a member, you will receive 22 issues of the *Communiqué* plus
the 24-page Annual Investors' Forecast edition for only $79.

In the letter, Alex makes and reviews recommendations
for the Oxford Trading Portfolio, which has garnered
national attention for its impressive track record.

The Hulbert Financial Digest tracks the returns of the
Oxford Trading Portfolio – and the returns of 180 other
investment letters – and found that the Oxford Trading
Portfolio's five-year risk-adjusted returns put it among
the top five investment newsletters in the country.

You will also receive the twice-weekly
Oxford Portfolio Update e-letter, which includes
timely investment updates on recommendations.

We normally offer this annual subscription for $149 – but
we're extending a special lower rate to readers of *The Secret of Shelter Island*.